MAY 2 2 2014

D0073179

Disco Dance

Disco Dance

Lori Ortiz

The American Dance Floor
Ralph G. Giordano (Series Editor)

 GREENWOOD

AN IMPRINT OF ABC-CLIO, LLC
Santa Barbara, California • Denver, Colorado • Oxford, England

SPRINGDALE PUBLIC LIBRARY
405 S. Pleasant
Springdale, AR 72764

Library of Congress Cataloging-in-Publication Data

Ortiz, Lori.
  Disco dance / Lori Ortiz.
    p. cm. — (The American dance floor)
  Includes bibliographical references and index.
    ISBN 978–0–313–37746–4 (hard copy : alk. paper) — ISBN 978–0–313–37747–1 (ebook)
1. Disco dancing. I. Title.
GV1796.D57O77 2011
793.3'3—dc22   2010052570

ISBN: 978–0–313–37746–4
EISBN: 978–0–313–37747–1

15 14 13 12 11   1 2 3 4 5

This book is also available on the World Wide Web as an eBook.
Visit www.abc-clio.com for details.

Greenwood
An Imprint of ABC-CLIO, LLC

ABC-CLIO, LLC
130 Cremona Drive, P.O. Box 1911
Santa Barbara, California 93116-1911

This book is printed on acid-free paper ∞

Manufactured in the United States of America

Copyright Acknowledgments

The author and the publisher are grateful to the following for granting permission to reprint from their materials:

"I feel real when you touch me." (YOU MAKE ME FEEL (MIGHTY REAL) Written by Sylvester James and James Wirrick © 1978 Sequins At Noon Music/ Wirrick Music Lyric Excerpt Used by Permission/All Rights Reserved.)

For AG, 1929–2010, with love

Contents

Series Foreword

From the Lindy hop to hip-hop, dance has helped define American life and culture. In good times and bad, people have turned to dance to escape their troubles, get out, and have a good time. From high school proms to weddings and other occasions, dance creates some of our most memorable personal moments. It is also big business, with schools, competitions, and dance halls bringing in people and their dollars each year. And as America has changed, so too has dance. The story of dance is very much the story of America. Dance routines are featured in movies, television, and videos; dance styles and techniques reflect shifting values and attitudes toward relationships; and dance performers and their costumes reveal changing thoughts about race, class, gender, and other topics. Written for students and general readers, *The American Dance Floor* series covers the history of social dancing in America.

Each volume in the series looks at a particular type of dance, such as swing, disco, Latin, folk dancing, hip-hop, ballroom, and country and western. Written in an engaging manner, each book tells the story of a particular dance form and places it in its historical, social, and cultural context. Thus each title helps the reader learn not only about a particular dance form but also about social change. The volumes are fully documented, and each contains a bibliography of print and electronic resources for further reading.

Introduction

In the disco era, from the mid-1970s to the early 1980s, people had a new desire to come together. Dancing was the acceptable public expression of that desire. In SoHo (South of Houston Street), New York City, artists were setting up shops in the factories left by failed industries. At least one such space, the Loft, became a microcosm of the disco ideal—a world of civil rights and relative equality. This book looks at various facets of disco dancing and aims to provide a feeling of the era's pluralism.

Reexamining disco from a distance of about 30 years, with an evolved perspective, has been more useful than I could have imagined. But the distance had its difficulties too. I found that some club and restaurant Web sites had all but erased their disco history. Even our metropolitan libraries had scarce material on disco and even less on disco dancing when I started researching. Too embarrassing? Disco dancing may take the prize for Most Misunderstood. Putting a confused era into words, and then writing the body's emanations of that era, has been a challenge. Having gone there, I could not have hoped for a more enjoyable journey, in which I could redux that era of hope and its jouissance. Necessarily, I add new perspective, as a woman of this century and as a dance writer.

Albert Goldman, who chronicled the scene in his 1978 book *Disco*, saw a new society of hard-core dance addicts at David Mancuso's Loft. He saw power generated by "outcasts." Sixty percent of the private room downtown typically comprised people of color, and Goldman exoticized the "erotic energy" he felt. DJ David Mancuso's unfamiliar,

polyrhythmic music awed him. Vince Aletti validated the new dancing that emerged from underground and gay clubs and named the
music "disco" in his weekly *Record World* column Disco File. New York
City in the 1970s *was* like a jungle. Aletti was excited about the new
music made, or selected by the DJ, for dancing. Mancuso's choices
were unfamiliar at the time and, most famously, "Soul Makossa" by
the African expatriate group Manu Dibango spoke to Aletti and the
dancers on the floor.

I begin with a scant catalog of some of the most remembered clubs
that populated New York City before and after the Loft. They served
as sanctuary and cheap entertainment for working people, people of
color, and gay people. Let me say, right from the beginning, that discos
were not necessarily the *all-inclusive* sanctuaries promised. The Loft
asserts itself as the ideal melting pot. It was (and is) a surviving DIY
space, perhaps because Mancuso resisted the commercialism that led
disco to its downfall.

This book is admittedly New York-centric. I grew up in the area, in
the era, and I know it best. As a New York City-based writer, the city
is the center of my universe. In my chapter "Wild West," I foray into
several other U.S. urban centers, most importantly, San Francisco, also
known as San Frandisco, but I leave in-depth mapping west of New
York to others.

In "Can't Stop the Music," I pursue the relationship between dancing and music, disco and camp. Live musicians modeled dance steps
while performing in dance halls, in music videos, and on TV dance
shows. Dancers inspired new songs. I veer outside of disco to show
the crossover between genres. For example, glam rock left its mark.
Soul begat disco. Motown divas, Bette Midler, and Barbara Streisand
nurtured the form.

"Dance the Night Away" looks at genres that fomented in 1970s discos. People wanted to dance together again. It was a national pastime.
Talented dancers could learn in the clubs and many furthered their
skills in dance studios. Dancers also learned from professionals and
amateurs on TV and on the street corners. Drugs and alcohol prevailed
in varying degrees in the clubs, as performance enhancers, but the
most serious dancers knew that sobriety would serve them best. In
the era, however, so many wanted to be stars, and drugs aided the illu-
sion. Dancers could reinvent themselves with costumes and with
learned or invented steps. Dancing gave voice to people who were

shy with words. They could participate in the sociality and community of the dance floor, speaking with their dancing bodies.

In "Those '70s Shows," I review several that shaped or best reflect on the disco era, beginning with the most pivotal *Saturday Night Fever*.

In conclusion, drugs and AIDS took their toll, reducing numbers on the floor, and closing clubs. Homophobia and white flight raged. It finally imploded with huge protests and a public "disco sucks" campaign, complete with patches to sew on your clothing to show protest and violent arsonist witch hunts. Did Grace Jones know that disco records would be burned as effigies in Chicago's Comisky Park when she fought back against the religious right's bigotry? Looking back from the twenty-first century, such violent backlash at people dancing and having fun looks completely outrageous. In retrospect, it was nothing but hot air, as dancing in clubs persists today on a different, healthier level. Generally, dancing emerged as a separate entity from the excessive drug use and sexual promiscuity that accompanied it back in those days.

If disco music and dancing helped people to forget and replace pain with pleasure, then the memories are scant and possibly distorted, when called upon later. Dancing demands something of us. Further, to pry words about it is a challenge for which we must suspend disbelief. That said, I offer this volume as a good read about a lost-and-found adventure, a telling of a decade of endangered memories.

I am most grateful for the open generosity of the people interviewed in the following pages who shared their experience with me trustingly. I would also like to thank the editors and especially series editor Ralph Giordano for his knowledge and support. I am grateful to my family and my most dutiful reader Amy Galowitz. Thanks to the International Hustle Dance Association, NY Hustle Congress, Miami Hustle and Salsa Competition, Holy Spirit Dance Club, Dance Critics Association, Facebook, Rhythm Lounge, Jeffrey Stoddard, Glen Weilgus, and HARO for connecting me with the Life. I would like to acknowledge Diane Tanchak, A.N.S. Digital, Bleeker Records, the New York Public Library, DJ History.com, the Central Park Dance Skaters Association, Karen Lynn Gorney, and the LGBT Center archive. Among the many people who shared memories of the era in casual conversation, constant Jeffrey Cyphers Wright never imposed. Jean LeBlanc, Richard Risio, Norma Markley, Elvis Mitchell, and countless others offered stories and advice. Thanks to the growing Web repositories Disco-disco.com and Discomusic.com, for the informative articles and endless threads of published comments that clarified my experience of the era. Last, thanks to former Hustle Champion Ron Bess for championing Hustle in *Dance Talk*. I apologize for the many omissions in this acknowledgment and in the book.

1

To the Disco

In the disco era, urban clubs brought new life into abandoned churches and theaters. Glitzy, glittery parties filled the commercialized, repurposed houses of worship and art. For example, the Sanctuary opened in the sooty, German Lutheran church near the entrance to the Lincoln Tunnel in Midtown Manhattan. The closed Fillmore East rock concert hall was reborn as the Saint. In casino-style, shopping mall-sized shells, professional hosts ran weekly or monthly dance parties with recurring themes or occasional themes like anniversaries or birthdays. The Limelight, a gothic-style former church, was a site for artists' late-night after-opening events. Uncle Sam's discos popped up along freeways as franchised fun centers, while at the other end of the scale, tiny clubs sprouted in basement dens and attics around the country.

Esprit de corps (a feeling of unity and togetherness) on the dance floor was the most important ingredient of a successful disco. That feeling of oneness was and is achieved through dancing. Although ritualistic, folkloric, and other dance forms strive for it, Unity is disco's nom de plume. Shared group feeling was tantamount to the total experience. Within that, disco often took form as protest dance in hopes of revolution; yet it is often judged by the bad times in which it occurred. The early 1970s general funk came about with the sinking economy, an unpopular war, and high crime in New York City. The me generation was in full swing. Efforts for black power, gay liberation, and women's liberation were salient. Disco dancing was part of the solution. It was humanity reminding us of its presence. In the ideal scenario,

chemicals were not needed to experience dancing's transformative
effect, just the dancer's natural adrenaline. That was the ideal, back
in the day.

Allies

The word *discotheque* is a *portmanteau*. In this case, disc and *bibliothèque*
(French for library) join to form a new word meaning record library.
The Parisian La Discothèque adopted the name when it opened in 1941
on the Rue de la Huchette in Paris (Jones 2000). After World War II, the
alliance between France and the United States resulted in a mingling
and trading of cultures. During the war, Nazi occupiers enjoyed the
French nightlife but not the jazz clubs. Because of the form's black,
American, and Jewish origins, jazz music and swing dancing were
among *verboten* art forms and leisure activities. So, it went underground.
Peter Braunstein, in his 1999 *American Heritage Journal* study of disco,
wrote in support of nightlife as cultural revolution. "The elements
that prevail during times of revolution—the exhilaration of collective
experience, the inversion of social roles, the supremacy of the present,
the triumph of imaginative life—can all be found in the dusk-to-dawn
alternative world of the nightclub" (Braunstein 1999, 43).

The French Resistance adopted jazz as an emblem. At the earliest
French clubs, drinks were served and patrons listened to jazz records.
In 1947, Paul Pacini's Parisian Whisky au Go-Go served up American
music and cocktails, which the French thought Americans preferred
over wine. "Go-Go" referred to the American get-up-and-go spirit.
Decades later, the affection was returned when Whisky au Go-Go
clubs opened in Chicago and Hollywood.

New York, New York

An infatuation with whiskey, jazz, and all things American fed into the
disco phenomenon but took some decades to actually arrive here.
Olivier Coquelin imported the French concept to New York, opening
Le Club in 1960 on Sutton Place and East Fifty-fifth Street in a converted parking garage. The elite clientele paid a $200 initiation fee plus
a $65 annual due. The entrance was discreet. Braunstein's source
described the interior as "a French playboy's dream of the ultimate
seduction pad" with a fireplace and stuffed hunting trophies, swords,

Regine was born Régine Zylberberg to Polish-Jewish parents in Belgium in 1929. She hid in a French convent during the war and rejoined her family afterward in Paris. Her father owned a bistro where she worked as a hostess. She dreamed of a place where she could pick and choose her guests. At 23, Regine landed a job as a hat-check girl at Whiskey au Go-Go. The playboys noticed her spirited energy and flaming red hair. She could sing and dance. Promoted to hostess and then manager, Regine laid down a linoleum floor and put in colored lights. She got rid of the juke-box and played records on two turntables to eliminate the gap between songs; she perceived the uncomfortable silence as rude and unwelcome for the patrons dancing or enjoying each other's company in the dimly lit space. Considered the very first disc jockey, or DJ, Regine created an atmosphere of boundlessness. The club's free-flowing intoxicants, alcohol, music, and love predated and enabled the coming of the disco era, where the pleasure principle ruled.

The wealthy European Rothschilds enjoyed Regine's renovations and in 1958 they helped finance a second Whiskey au Go-Go in the Latin Quarter of Paris, but everyone called it Chez Regine. It is considered the first discotheque. Bridget Bardot, Rudolph Nureyev, and Premier Georges Pompidou were among the visitors. One night the cast of *West Side Story* came in and taught everyone the twist. Patrons bought bottles of liquor instead of cocktails. At another Paris club Regine opened, New Jimmy's, she held themed fetés or "happenings" at which the patrons were the performers. Women wore Hollywood-style white satin dresses for her Jean Harlow Party. A white carpet was rolled out for them to enter the club from their Rolls Royces, which were painted white for the night (Baumgold 1977).

and tapestries on the walls. There were other elite discotheques including El Morocco, which Lyndon Johnson used as a fund-raising headquarters for his presidential campaign. Il Mio and L'Interdit were also popular, as was Shepheard's. The décor was themed and continental. In 1964, New York teens went to the Peppermint Lounge, a.k.a. Temple of the Twist, hoping to see the Beatles twist after their

Rudolf Nureyev and Margot Fonteyn celebrate after work in a disco, 1965.
(Associated Press)

performance on the Ed Sullivan show. Only Ringo danced (Giordano, *Social Dancing in America* 2007). There, Joey Dee and the Starliters performed "Peppermint Twist." The Lounge was a venue for onstage musicians and not technically a discotheque. While the Beatles were capturing the hearts of millions of teens, the disco phenomenon gave form, fulfillment, and self-expression to the extreme and marginal elements of the same society. Soon, people of all ages, races, and socioeconomics, including glamorous celebrities, felt the beat, buzz, vibrations, and wanted to dance and participate.

Sybil Burton, Richard Burton's first wife, opened the Sutton Place Arthur's, after the couple split in 1965. Brought up in a Welsh mining family, she welcomed not only moneyed and celebrity clientele but also working women with "style, sensibility, and spirit." She was inspired by the London club Ad Lib's British mod sensibility. Arthur's opened on the heels of the Beatles' arrival in the United States. In fact, Burton took the name "Arthur" from George Harrison's funny answer to a reporter's question, "What do you call your haircut?" in the film *A Hard Day's Night* (Braunstein 1999).

Discotheque decor grew more elaborate in the late 1960s, facilitated by new and better technology. The enormous, repurposed spaces required bigger, sometimes, ear-shattering sound. Artist Andy Warhol created a portable system he called the Exploding Plastic Inevitable. It included The Velvet Underground band and looped Warhol films including *Eat*, *Banana*, *Vinyl*, and *Couch*. Dancers performed illuminated by the projector's beams, with flickering light reflected off the all-important mirrored disco ball. (Rotating mirrored balls had been used as far back as the 1930s to decorate dance marathons.) Coquelin opened Cheetah at Fifty-third Street and Broadway in 1966 and featured Warhol's EPI. The club had an 8,000-square-foot dance floor and conveniences like a clothing boutique for guests who needed something better to wear for the night out. Dancers did the Cheetah Shuffle, a line dance, calling out numbered steps. Cheetah featured live bands, but it is one example of the way the club experience expanded spectacularly. They catered to patrons with disposable income who were seeking numbing spectacle and sensory overload. Also, the hallucinogenic visuals and flowing nonstop sound availed the dancing or groovin' substance user. The clubs were a venue, not just for musicians and recording artists, but for visual artists too. Filmmaker Jonas Mekas's Expanded Cinema set projected film footage and color slides to music. Much later, multimedia would be popularized in music videos and MTV.

East Village Clubs

Warhol rented The Polish National Home, called Dom's (Polish for home), in the 19–25 St. Marks Place and converted row houses to stage EPI happenings. The next year, in 1967, the counterculture Electric Circus opened upstairs. Flyers invited club goers to come stoned. Costumes could be purchased on the premises. Dances and circus acts like flame swallowing were performed on pedestals. The performers modeled behavior and fostered a sense of unity among the revelers.

The East Village Mudd Club, October 30, 1979. (Photo by Allan Tannenbaum)

The crowd moved while fascinated, tripping on mind-expanding drugs, or visiting private fantasies. They were creating as well as responding to the spectacle. Other East Village clubs like the Mudd Club and Pyramid followed, staging rock bands. They shared disco elements like wild costumes, drugs, gender ambiguity, and imperatives of abandon and fun. (Pyramid had and still has a disco night.) Partygoers hopped from one to the other. Although the three above-mentioned clubs could each be associated with an address, some clubs moved from one location to another, inhabiting two or three different shells while in existence. Landlords wanted a share in the profits from the successful ventures and raised rents in the unregulated commercial spaces. Clubs then pulled up their (mostly shallow) roots and sought cheaper addresses. Sometimes a change in management or location was the beginning of the end. Other times, new management would attract a different crowd. Conversely, with changing interiors, operators could stretch out the club's life expectancy, holding the attention of a particular crowd, by changing with the times. Theme parties, musical and visual thrills, generated buzz.

When disco emerged as a full-blown cultural phenomenon and a mainstream entertainment, the shortening of the imported term disco-theque came to stand for the phenomenon and era. At its center was the club or discotheque, where social dancing reigned, fueled by the music that was made for it. Cultural outsiders—black, gay, and Latino inventors of the style—disseminated the dance throughout and beyond the disco era.

New York's 1926 Prohibition era cabaret law states that unless an establishment that serves food and drink has a cabaret license, three or more people cannot dance. This was intended to crack down on speakeasies. The law persisted, although in retrospect it is understood as serving racist fears of uprisings and multiracial cavorting in the Harlem jazz clubs.

Since then, and possibly more than ever in the disco era, people like David Mancuso found creative ways to share their love of dancing and music.

The Loft

In 1970, David Mancuso started having rent parties at his second floor loft on lower Broadway. Admittance was by invitation only, and donations of three or four dollars were taken at the door. The unofficial dance hall was simply called "the Loft." The parties were the model for later downtown discos, notably Gallery and then the legendary Paradise Garage. Mancuso was known for his innovative acoustics and for his ability to create a truly mixed crowd of fun-seekers. They described his inspiring musical programs as "perfectionist." The group energy that developed in response to his improvised playlist is renown. Mancuso's individualist scores depended on his observation of the mood on the dance floor. Dancers would form a circle and take their turn performing in the middle, a custom they brought in from uptown street corners. Says Mancuso, who still holds underground downtown loft parties 30 years later, "It was all about the dancer, not the DJ." But he set a standard for later DJs who had much more sophisticated technology at their disposal. He had a wide-ranging taste in his mix and introduced dancers, musicians, and music producers to little-known artists. With his private parties, Mancuso could stay within the law without having to get special licenses. Snacks were on hand, but no alcohol was served, and dancers discretely used psychedelic drugs. This format—punch and fruit bowl refreshments and bring-your-own optionally altered mood—was copied in countless discos around the city and beyond.

David Mancuso did not offer a Loft playlist because of the improvisational nature of his programs. When asked what music he played, he answered "dance music." The myth surrounding him includes a mix of exotic and not so exotic music, for example, a guest brought him Barrabas's "Wild Safari" and "Woman." He played Willie Henderson's "Dance Master" and Led Zeppelin. Most famously, he introduced "Soul Makossa." Vince Aletti reported having heard these songs when he visited the Loft Christmas Day night, 1976. The writer admitted he is not a night-bird and did not frequent the Loft. He probably arrived early before things heated up.

"Anambra": Ozo

"Don't Leave Me This Way": Thelma Houston

"Gotta Get It": Tony Valor Sounds Orchestra

"It Ain't Reggae (But It's Funky)": Instant Funk

"It Don't Have To Be Funky": Salsoul Orchestra

"I've Learned My Burns": Spiders Webb

"Keep On Dancing": [The] Jacksons

"Love In C Minor": Cerrone

"Open Sesame": Kool & the Gang

"Sunrise": Ultrafunk

(Aletti, *The Disco Files: 1973–78*, 2009, 251)

To some, New York, and particularly Manhattan, was a scary place in the 1970s. Most white people did not go to Harlem. Forty-second Street was a succession of peep show parlors and XXX-rated movie theaters. Live sex trade was open and ubiquitous around midtown. In 1975, when 5,000 police officers were suddenly laid off because of financial crisis, it was open season for looting and crime on New York streets. Meanwhile, artists were making spacious refuges south of Houston Street in SoHo's abandoned factories. In one such factory, Mancuso held his dances.

Complaints from Loft neighbors and a *New York Times* article brought the police, and finally Mancuso was forced out. The party moved to Ninety-nine Prince Street, after a year's hiatus, with an afternoon Easter party in 1975. Reporting in the *Village Voice,* Aletti said it was like a family reunion. Best of all, the Loft may have fulfilled disco's ideal of gay, straight, black, and white comingling. Back in the day, young, gay, black males heated up the dance floor, sometimes performing within rings of onlookers. Mancuso based his list of invitees on personal preference. How will this potential guest affect the dance energy? As an exclusive private party (for 500), the Loft was not *required* to have a mixed crowd.

In 1970, when the Loft opened, a New York State Liquor Authority rule was in effect, stating that it was illegal to sell alcohol to homosexuals. Bar owners had to make sure some women were present, and they frowned upon male patrons with tight clothes or limp wrists. In order to stay open, gay bars paid the Mafia for protection against police harassment. The next year, with pressure from the Gay Activists Alliance, Mayor Lindsay repealed that ruling. In the 1970s, many New Yorkers were divided or conflicted. Some were fascinated with homosexuality, and some were terrified of it.

Gay Gotham

Seymour Seiden and Shelley Bloom founded several pre-Stonewall, illegal gay-gathering places in the West Village, like Salvation on Sheridan Square. In the West Village, the owners' monthly $1,000 payoffs were a friendly gesture and bought extra protection. Beat policemen would avert their eyes and ears to the large, illegal congregations of men dancing with men, outward displays of illegal homosexuality, drinking, drugging, and noisy carousing that spilled out onto the sidewalks at closing time. The night they missed that payment, Stonewall happened. The 1969 raid is the historic event that opened the floodgates for gay liberation. Before Stonewall, gays danced in mixed company. They were invited because they could move to the music uninhibitedly. Gay culture is a physical one, and the men aimed for a fit, attractive, seductive bodily expression. They were accepted in clubs and were thrilled to have a place in which to socialize and behave in a way that felt natural. Gay men were actually sought after for their propensity for unabashed party fun. A gay couple or individual typically had more disposable income; men's earnings were higher. Club admission fees were not a problem for hard-working, hard-playing men. Many did not have family at home, and the dancers on the floor substituted.

In June of 1969, police raided the Stonewall Inn, a gay bar on Christopher Street with two dance floors, for serving liquor without a license. (Establishments that were known to draw a homosexual patronage were denied liquor licenses in those days.) According to Tim Lawrence, in his book *Love Saves the Day*, the bar stood out because of a missed payment. The patrons rebelled. One transgender activist, the late Sylvia Rivera, is credited with instigating the famous uprising that touched off the Gay Liberation Movement. A group of Puerto Rican drag queens formed a chorus line and sang, "We are the Stonewall girls . . ." while kicking their legs up. Gay male patrons and supporters gathered and threw coins, bottles, and rocks at the police. Rivera was taken into the paddy wagon, while the men in blue raided the bar. Of the men who had been dancing and drinking, some were more timid and were still inside. They got pushed back along with raiding police, who had barricaded themselves inside when the door was locked. A small fire started and police responded with a hosing. Accounts vary. There was little media coverage, but the *Post* estimated that more than 1,000 gathered. Most call Stonewall the start of the gay liberation. The Mattachine Society's earlier efforts to fight discrimination cannot be discounted, but Stonewall was revolutionary. There were 50 or 60 gay groups up until then, and over 1,500 formed in the next year. In 1999 the bar became the first gay or lesbian site to be listed on the National Register of Historic Places. Stonewall is remembered annually in gay pride celebrations throughout the United States.

Discotheques were touted as places where discrimination was left at the door and particularly exclusion of minorities. Among groups often excluded based on class, race, and sexual preference, the best dancers could be found. They were sought after by club owners like Mancuso and party planners who micromanaged crowd composition. In the process of natural, or outright, selection, there was a certain amount of segregation in the club nightscape.

Potential club operators snapped up abandoned city structures. Gay men, perhaps more than any other group, found sanctuary en masse in the underground gathering places.

Sanctuary (from *Klute*). Legend has it that Jane Fonda, a club goer and Women's Liberation activist, was upset that only men were in Sanctuary and insisted on bringing women extras into this scene. (Photofest)

Sanctuary opened as a mixed club. Patrons of every race and class sat in pews on the sides facing inward and danced in the central nave. The DJ booth was on the altar. Seiden and Bloom (a.k.a. Seymour and Shelley) bought the club in 1970, and a newly liberated gay crowd flocked to the West Forty-third Street former German Lutheran church. It is widely considered the first openly gay-dominated discotheque. It closed in 1972 after a series of drug busts. Bloom was found murdered in his Gramercy Park home two weeks before the closing (Post 1978, 81).

On the Upper West Side, after Stonewall, Steve Ostrow opened an important gay Mecca in the Ansonia Hotel. Patrons stayed for days at Continental Baths and danced to nonstop music spun by beginners Levan and Frankie Knuckles. They would become two of the most remembered disco era DJs. Bette Midler and Barry Manilow debuted live at the Baths. Midnight shows featured Manhattan Transfer, Talley Brown, Jackie Curtis, Holly Woodlawn, and other stars of the day. Admission fee was $4.50 in 1972. Women were admitted but were requested to leave after the show. Food, sex, and all needs were met.

Clothing could be purchased, but patrons danced wrapped in towels, which inevitably fell off.

Le Jardin opened in 1973 and attracted a crowd that was "essentially gay with a smallish quota of fashionable women and straights," says the team at disco-disco.com (LeBash n.d.). The upscale club, housed in the midtown Diplomat Hotel, had two levels: a roof penthouse and basement. The waiters wore roller skates. The National Association of Discotheque Disc Jockeys crowned Gloria Gaynor Queen of Discotheques after her Le Jardin performance on March 3, 1975.

Hairdressers, wait staff, barmen, and other service people went out Sunday night. The $10 admission charge included two drinks, breakfast, and a free record. On Saturday night, admission was $10 for men and $20 for women. There was no loyalty issue—if there were too many women in the club, the gay men would head elsewhere. If gay men were thought to have an edge on music, dance, fun, and chic, the unfortunate term "fag hags" was coined for their many women friends.

Out gay men then found refuge at the Tenth Floor on Twenty-third Street, Gallery in SoHo, and dive bars along the West Side Highway. The dancing was seductive and dancers made off to the bathrooms, stairwells, West Side Meatpacking District alleys, or the Hudson River Piers for more intimate, pre-dawn trysts. One-night stands and frequently changing sexual partners were common. Instead of psychedelic drugs, drugs that enhanced sensuality like poppers (amyl nitrate), Quaaludes, and cocaine were plentiful in 1970s gay discos. The men used drugs to heighten sensuality and lower levels of inhibition. The resulting promiscuity and unprotected, public sex accelerated the spread of AIDS among gay men in New York. Scientific study of the virus and its prevention had yet to be undertaken.

West Chelsea was desolate and dangerous in the mid-1970s. Murderers lurked in doorways, and muggings were common. "Homeless" emerged as a catchword. People shut out of institutions roamed the streets and slept in boxes. They encountered few beat cops or social workers looking for them. In 1977 there were 1,557 murders in the city, reported Police Commissioner Raymond Kelly in a panel discussion held at the thirtieth anniversary of the Son of Sam's rampage (Kelly 2007). Many women stayed in, afraid to go out. They were dispensable at clubs, where men now freely congregated without their cover protection. A few women were privileged to join gay clubs or were invited as special guests.

Flamingo opened above Gallery and drew an elite group of wealthy gay professionals. Gay men consider it the origin of White and Black circuit parties. 12 West was another popular destination in a former flower warehouse at Christopher Street and the West Side Highway. The crowd there was mixed-race and more casual. It was a family place where disco was king before the backlash, said DJ Robbie Leslie. "It was a wonderful melting pot of gay culture." Where Flamingo was more about hooking up, 12 West was really about dancing all night. No alcohol was served. It had a square dance floor, with 10 or more disco balls above it, flanked with banquettes on three sides. 12 West was open three days a week. In 1979 Leslie was one of two alternating DJs.

Former Broadway dancer Michael Fesco's Flamingo, around the corner from the Loft, was more upscale. Membership cost $600 per year. Three recommendations were needed. The smaller Loft-inspired Gallery, with its more urban crowd, had moved to the corner of Houston and Mercer in a ground floor space just below Flamingo. When the Saint opened in 1980, however, Flamingo, 12 West, and other gay clubs went out of business.

Saint or Garage

Members of the Saint and Paradise Garage were amicable camps of gay revelers in the 1980s. Bruce Mailman owned the New St. Marks Baths in the East Village. It was a large gathering of men in towels, leather and chains, or bandages. Mailman said relations at the baths were "look, touch, but that's it," in a videotaped interview (The Saint 2007). He had unsuccessfully fought its closure when the baths were shut down in 1985 by the City Department of Health. He bought several East Village Theaters including the Fillmore East at 105 Second Avenue. He created the Saint on that site in 1980. Mailman died of AIDS in 2008 at age 55.

The Saint was the ultimate space-age fantasyland with its planetarium dome and spectacular light shows. Famed, tribal, Saint Black parties did not end when the club closed. They continued as annual underground events where cameras were checked at the door. F. Scott Bromley, a Saint architect and charter member, said, "You didn't find out about it in the *New York Times*. It was word of mouth" (Bromley 2008).

The first discotheque to host a weekly circuit party may have been the legendary Saint. When it opened, it became the destination of choice for the upper echelons of gay dancers. And it was there that they saw the as yet unnamed Acquired Immune Deficiency Syndrome or AIDS on the drawn faces of their chosen, dancing family. They called it the gay cancer. It spread to gay urban communities around the nation and elsewhere. Club membership was hit hard and the Saint closed in 1988; but circuit parties continued, then serving largely as fund-raising events for the Gay Men's Health Crisis.

Annual extravaganzas marked New York's Gay Pride weekend, around the anniversary of Stonewall. The nondenominational holiday Thanksgiving was also reason for a huge celebration. Black parties and White parties were institutionalized at the Saint, says William (Billy) Carroll, a busy DJ who began in 1975. They celebrated male rites around the vernal equinox and the February full moon, respectively. It was not long before the idea of themed parties and celebrations took hold in the mainstream at Studio 54 and big-name clubs from Minneapolis to Montreal and beyond. The scope of the event, and the muscled look of the invitees, qualified it as a circuit party. People jetted to the Saint from other cities to attend bashes that extended through the weekend. After the Saint closed, dance-a-thons and weeklong parties moved to convention centers and hotel ballrooms. Drugs, sexual freedom, body consciousness, and unity fueled the dancing that kept people coming. The huge circuit parties were like vacations and consisted of people who could afford to travel.

Gay and straight sadomasochists have been drawn to Black parties for the sexual focus. Steven Weinstein documented the scene in the gay New York weekly *Blade*. Recent Black Party guest Michael Weems told Weinstein that the costumed men looked dignified and elegant. David Nimmons called the atmosphere of the revival party seeking to replicate the Saint's, a "primal dark energy . . . a libidinal commonality." Violent sex in the balcony and backrooms, deaths, injuries, and drug fallouts were not uncommon. The Saint's fabled live sex shows included bestiality and boas. Wretched and debauched to some, the clandestine rites reached ecstatic and spiritual heights for the participants. Costumes included leather, masks, rubber wetsuits, chaps, and birthday suits. At the Saint in the 1970s, and for today's men, the rites strip away feelings of shame, leaving observable dignity. Carroll said, "The man from Ohio might feel out of place" (B. Carroll 2008).

The most famous element at the Saint was a 14-foot-tall, high-tech-looking launch-pad structure that could levitate 12 feet off the floor.

In the 1970s, people like Anita Bryant and others thought that homosexuals were particularly libidinous and therefore immoral. Gays did not have a monopoly on the idea of multiple partners and increased sexual pleasure. Across the nation, *heterosexual* couples were experimenting with open marriages and promiscuous, liberated behavior. Sex itself had come out of the closet, and Alex Comfort's 1972 *The Joy of Sex* was the sensational instruction manual. The ancient Indian *Kama Sutra* was another popular guide. (The year 1977 brought Edmund White and Dr. Charles Silverstein's *The Joy of Gay Sex*.) Heterosexual, married swingers swapped partners in clubs like the bacchanalian Plato's Retreat. That club featured a giant mattress full of squirming bodies turning every way for sexual attention, as it is notably portrayed in the Spike Lee movie *Summer of Sam*.

The removal of clothing in clubs was not restricted to homosexuals. Gay and straight disco dancers hoped to reduce inhibition or heighten the body's sensual and sexual pleasure by using drugs. Some recreational drugs had a lasting effect for marathons. Some were less potent and cheaper than the party drugs of later decades.

It was larger than a planetarium's. Projectors mounted on top threw indirect light and stars onto the dome-shaped ceiling. Members and guests called the central projector affectionately "the tree" or "the mothership." In September 1980, on the Saint opening night, the wood floor had been painted black, which added to the celestial, otherworldly atmosphere. The floor, walls, and ceiling blended into one. Everything was dark, with what looked like moving constellations above. Inside the powerful theatrical effects, dancers imagined themselves in a heavenly atmosphere, outdoors, under the stars, and free from earthly restraints. "The gays like to be swept up in the whole thing," said gay DJ Robbie Leslie, who was there on opening night and worked many parties, including the last. The control booth was the only point of orientation (Leslie 2010).

Mailman and designer Charles Terrel intended it to look limitless and disorienting. The circular dance floor was 48,000-square-feet wide. Joseph Spencer and Spencer Designs specified 1,500 light fixtures,

Studio 54's 2nd anniversary party showing DJ booth (on upper left) and bridge, a later addition used for performance and for patrons looking down on the dance floor, April 26, 1979. (Photo by Allan Tannenbaum)

including a police beacon, pin spots, and wall washers. A thousand focused on a scrim that covered the dome ceiling. The lighting plan stated that "the customer is the focus, silhouetted and highlighted wherever he goes." A 36-inch, motorized, mirrored disco ball dropped from a five-foot hatch at the top. The 336 speakers, arranged in four groups, were pointed directly at the dancers.

Metal grate staircases led to a balcony lounge and coatroom. Four hundred people could be up above, looking down. According to Leslie, it was a minority using the balcony for sex. It was not like a wall-to-wall orgy. For most, it was a matter of going out, having a good time, and going home happy. A normal, nine-hour weekend night regime might have included the drugs angel dust, marijuana, cocaine, mescaline, THC, poppers, and finally downers like Quaaludes, Nembutal, and/or prescription antidepressants. Black, White, and other themed party nights lasted many hours (or days) longer.

When AIDS caused patronage to dwindle, invitations came back stamped "Addressee Deceased." Mailman started straight nights in desperation. Leslie, one of several DJs working at the Saint closing party in May 1988, is still going strong today (see pp. 78–81).

The Saint crowd was 99 percent white. At the Paradise Garage the membership was urban and racially mixed. An average night would draw about 15 percent women. Carroll is a Garage loyalist because that club and DJ Larry Levan spawned a new genre of music called "garage." That sound developed into the house or dance music prevalent in nightclubs of the next decades. Levan's style and the club platform was a direct descendant of the Loft and was nurtured at the Gallery, where Levan did lighting and worked with DJ Nicky Siano.

Carroll, bored with the music and nightlife in Hartford, Connecticut, came into the city as a teenager and helped put out the fresh fruit at the Gallery. It was one of a handful of juice bars downtown where underage kids could go. Everything had acid in it, he said. Drugs were injected into the oranges. But the dancers at the Gallery were phenomenal—Latino boys from the boroughs. They were straight, but the drugs escalated their sexual energy; and if they had not found a woman by morning, they would be willing. The down low thing was happening then, and the boys were called "hitters."

Michael Brody opened the 3,000-square-foot Garage in 1976. Its membership community of gay men expressed their relatively newfound liberation, said Brody's former partner, the late Mel Cheren, founder of West End Records, in his autobiography *Keep on Dancin': My Life and the Paradise Garage* (Cheren 2000).

The Garage ranks of devoted followers amicably rival the Saint's. Both memberships were coveted and awarded by recommendation, as were Loft invitations. Men kept their shirts on at the Garage. There, it was all about the music and hooking up for sex was secondary, according to Carroll. "Real movies, not porn" were shown in its theater. Free punch, fruit, and snacks were served. The club was open all year-round and attracted a local crowd. Most remember the heat, both figuratively and literally. It was hot and sweaty in the summer, with no air conditioning. Levan's sound would read the dancing, cheering crowd until 1987 when Brody became too ill to run the club and closed it. Levan died five years later, ill and drug-addled.

The Saint closed the next year. AIDS took its toll. Because the voluminous club was only in operation on Saturday and holiday nights, it was not an efficient use of prime real estate in the gentrifying East Village. It was dormant in the summer when its wealthier customers flocked to Fire Island.

Fire Island

Disco dancers remember Ice Palaces in three midtown locations. One
was a skating rink on an upper floor. But many consider the Ice Palace
in the Cherry Grove section of Fire Island the first gay disco. "Groove
in the Grove," they advertised a different kind of disco. High Tea
was served from four to six every afternoon. White sand edges that
thin strip of beach community accessible only by ferry from Long
Island. It is about an hour's train journey east of New York City. Copa
was another popular club right on the beach. It was set on fire in 1978
and burned to the ground. One Ice Palace guest commented on the
Web site discomusic.com that Ice Palace DJ Roy Thode played "Disco
Inferno" meanwhile. Thode committed suicide in 1982, said John
Ceglia, a DJ from Buffalo, whom Thode had brought in to Ice Palace
in 1980. Ceglia was rotating in the NYC downtown discos with Leslie,
Thode, Jim Burgess, and others. The Cherry Grove Ice Palace celebrated
50 years in 2007. Dancers went there on Friday and Saturday night and
then moved over to Pavilion for Sunday Tea Dance. Pavilion opened on
the site of the Sandpiper after that club closed in 1979.

In the 1970s, gay New Yorkers including Cheren and Brody took
house shares in a section called The Pines. The Fire Island clubs were
important and trendsetting because of their A-list, music industry
clientele. The crowd at Sandpiper was 95 percent male. Most were
Flamingo, Loft, 12 West, or Tenth Floor dancers with summer shares
on the island.

Sandpiper was a restaurant in the daytime and a disco from midnight to 4 a.m. Glass doors led outside to decks overlooking the water.
Its capacity was 500 to 600. On Sundays, Botel held a popular Tea
Dance. Afterward, dancers would head over to Sandpiper as a final,
weekend destination. DJ Robbie Leslie presided at "Our Halloween,"
a special Last Dance on Saturday, October 31. Reservations were
required. A bus departed New York City at 10 p.m. Breakfast was
served, and the boat returned at dawn. Leslie had embarked on his
30-plus-year DJ career at Sandpiper.

Hard-working men like architect Scott Bromley and friends spent
every weekend at Sandpiper and Pavilion. Gays established weekend
Fire Island circuit parties at a disco without walls, called simply
Beach. Bromley and Jacobson designed the open-air beach party in
1979. It was set up on regular Saturday nights and lasted from sunset

Before opening Studio 54, Rubell and Schrager operated the Queens club Enchanted Garden. Residential neighbors had them evicted on June 23, 1976. (Photo by Allan Tannenbaum)

to sunrise. They anchored very tall wooden construction planks in the sand and topped them with translucent flags made of yards of red and blue mosquito netting. More planks were laid tongue and groove on the sand to make a serviceable dance floor. Seating areas were created with inner tubes covered in soft cotton medical gauze.

The Beach parties melded into the Gay Men's Health Crisis Morning Party, a circuit party in remembrance of those who died. It was a great fund-raiser and lasted for 16 years annually until too many were overdosing on drugs.

Women started moving on to Fire Island and filled in the void, buying homes left by men who died. "But now the Grove is returning," said long-time resident and Grove fireman Dominick Desantis, "with the young guys coming back" (Jordan n.d.).

Everybody Dance Now

Heterosexuals edged in as spectators in gay clubs, dressing up in bizarre and unisex costumes in order to get in. "Disco promised euphoria, glamour, and decadence at a reasonable price" (Braunstein 1999). Recorded music reduced overhead. A DJ cost as little as $50 a night. Meanwhile, popular music was turning toward more dance-oriented rhythms and longer songs. Disco had coalesced as a multipart package of dance, music, and the discotheque. Disco was by no means mainstream until the movie *Saturday Night Fever* brought it to a safe distance on the big screen. Meanwhile, the new, theater-district discos attracted celebrities, became famous themselves, and multiplied. The disco ethos spread upward and outward.

Regine's

Regine moved to New York in 1975 and found an apartment in the Delmonico Hotel on West Fifty-fourth Street. There, on the ground floor, she opened the posh, U.S. flagship Regine's a year later. A $600 membership guaranteed free entrance with up to eight guests, and by opening night 2,000 memberships were sold. The numbers grew to 20,000. Regine's featured parties with international themes and a disco contest judged by Andy Warhol. The crowd was a mix that ranged in age and stature—well-dressed nobodies rubbed shoulders with famous artists and designers, jet-setting politicians, and royalty—as in earlier, chic midtown clubs like Arthur's and the soon-to-be neighboring Studio 54. At the height of her empire, 25 Regine's were counted in jet-set destinations around the world. Regine's perfumes and other luxury product endorsements followed. She developed a *prêt-à-danser* collection and dancersize classes. Meanwhile, she recorded a 12-inch single "Je Survivrai" ("I Will Survive"). Prism Records released it in 1979.

Regine perpetuated the suggestion of disco glamour that originated in creative, artistic, "beat," post-war watering holes. With her oversize personality and ambition, she took credit for saving New York from bankruptcy and called herself "The Queen of Hearts, Clubs, and Diamonds" (Grigoriadis 1999, 1).

Regine did not get a cabaret license, and people wanted to dance. The Giuliani administration was enforcing the outdated cabaret law that prohibited drinking and dancing under one roof. At Studio 54 they were not so concerned about lawbreaking. People moved on. This was due, in part, to the fickle nature of club goers whose loyalties were limited to the newest thrill. "She wasn't giving out Quaaludes to movie stars, she didn't have bartenders with their shirts off. She didn't have what people wanted when the times changed," said *Interview* editor Bob Colacello (Grigoriadis 1999, 5).

Studio 54

Clubs for stars and stargazers, like Studio 54, also thrived on unity and the disco's democratic ethos. The atmosphere, however, was not like the disco set for *Saturday Night Fever*. Filming had begun a month before "Studio" opened on April 26, 1977. The Studio fantasy was feel good fame, rubbing shoulders with the stars, and sharing their light. While a virtual Brooklyn teen was redeemed through dance at 2001 Odyssey, the ultra cool cavorted in a super-elite bacchanal for the in-crowd. Warhol and his coterie of friends, assistants, and muses worked and played in The Factory, a studio he rented in various New York city locations, including the Dezer building near Union Square. Warholian pop merged club culture and the visual arts. Andy was often photographed there and is part of the Studio 54 legend.

"We knew [Studio] was going to be a household word," said Bromley who renovated the old Galileo Opera House on West Fifty-third Street as Studio for owners Steve Rubell and Ian Schrager. Maurice Brahms (of Infinity and later Underground) was involved in the founding.

The architects first removed the seats and created a level floor. "Everybody wants to be on the stage," Bromley told me (Bromley 2008). Then they redesigned it every fall. The second year they installed a moving bridge on which people danced and Diana Ross once sang. Black Astro Turf was the flooring. "This was the black age." The lighting design called for low-voltage motorcycle lights and neon. The columns had circulating, tracing lights that went up and down and changed colors like those on police cars.

The club was on the ground floor, and red velvet ropes cordoned off an area of the sidewalk in front of it for the expected throngs wanting to get in. The statuesque and flamboyant Jamaican-born singer/song-writer Grace Jones partied in costume at Studio 54 along with Warhol, other art stars, celebrities, fashionable folk, models, and good-looking nobodies. Some journalists, gossip columnists, and paparazzi were allowed in. Part owner Rubell purposely initiated the stringent door policy. He took time to personally winnow the most beautiful and famous, to create a logjam that would only inspire continued attempts. Attractive hopefuls waiting outside, at least, gave the impression that it was the place to be.

Through the glaze, a world was created where everyone was beauti-ful. Those would-bes that the doorperson or Rubell deemed glamorous

Dancer with shirt in hand at Studio 54 on April 15, 1978. (Photo by Allan Tannenbaum)

enough to enter could immediately balloon and glow with a sense self-worth, adding to the general glowing atmosphere. The admittance fee was the doorperson's prerogative; often Rubell himself was on hand. The most sought-after celebrity on show might pay nothing or hundreds of dollars. Once inside, the hedonistic haze of the fog machine, the flashing lights of the dance floor, the beat of the music and movement rendered everyone equal.

A large, pink sculpted relief roundel of a "Man on the Moon With a Coke Spoon" was lowered toward the dance floor every midnight. Staff moved a hinged appendage, a spoon smattered with painted white grains, in toward the giant face. The crowd cheered and screamed at what, today, seems like a silly ritual. In retrospect, it fueled the cultish fervor and glorified the drug itself. Cocaine was the choice at Studio and the cause célèbre.

Bianca Jagger wore a Halston dress and entered on a white horse for her thirty-second birthday party in May 1977. Jimmy Carter's mother, Michael Jackson, Martha Graham, Elton John, Truman Capote, and Mae West were among the guests. The party famously established Studio as the go-to celebrity club. John Blair and Jason hosted gay Sundays at Studio 54.

The basement VIP room and the upstairs balcony were the place for a little privacy and a lot of wild debauchery. In December 1978, federal agents raided the club and arrested Schrager for cocaine possession. One year later, another raid returned more drugs and piles of cash in black trash bags. The owners had skimmed $2.5 million. They were fined $20,000 each and jailed for tax evasion.

Diana Ross and Richard Gere were among the guests at a going away party. There was little to dispirit revelers in fantasyland. But the partying fizzled out after a second try with a new owner. The club had imploded, and without its unbelievable amounts of drugs and Rubell's talent, attendance dwindled. In 1986 it closed for good. Its fame is remembered in a new, triple-sized Las Vegas remake where anyone can get in for the price of admission.

Palladium

Meanwhile, Rubell and Schrager had irons in the fire. They hired architect Arata Isozaki to renovate the interior of an old movie house on Fourteenth Street and Third Avenue, which had served more recently as a pool hall and then a rock concert venue. The beautiful Rococo shell had fallen into disrepair, but Isozaki used the architecture as a design element along with new, high-tech installations in his Palladium interior. A romantic metal staircase was lighted from underneath, through round glass portals, like those outside the basements of city buildings. Upstairs were comfortable bleachers for resting and looking down at the sea of flesh. A curtain opened to enlarge the dance floor. Former patrons remember a four-walled house with scenes of the Brooklyn *Saturday Night Fever* club 2001 Odyssey. That set was raised to open up the floor. Palladium had banks of video monitors that came down from the ceiling. They screened MTV dance shows and had live performers dancing on the speakers (discomusic.com).

As convicted felons, Schrager and Rubell had trouble getting a liquor license, but by naming the new owners as The Muidallap Corporation, it could be accomplished in time for the grand opening in May 1985. An A-list of fashion designers and artists attended the party, including the 33-year-old Christopher Reeve, a.k.a. Superman, who was left paralyzed 10 years later due to a horseback-riding accident. Some of the artists made works for the club. Basquiat created a 40-foot mural. Keith Haring painted on phone booths and water coolers. Francesco Clemente decorated the vaulted ceilings.

That year, the anonymous Guerilla Girls formed a group that famously protested the exclusion of women artists from museums and galleries. It did not take long for them to notice that the club had no works by women. In apology, the owners invited the group to curate a show. "100 Women" opened on October 15. In the following years, the club would host benefits for Alvin Ailey American Dance Theater, Twyla Tharp, and The Actors Studio. Parties for Senator Daniel Patrick Moynihan's daughter, Madonna, and Keith Haring are some of the storied events. In the 1990s, the club was a favorite place for Latin dancing on Thursday nights. Patrons remember innovative dances of the day, born on that floor. It outlived Rubell, who died of AIDS in 1989 at the age of 46.

El Palladium

In 1947, promoter Frank Pagani brought Tito Puente downtown to the Alma Dance Studio on Fifty-third Street. Holocaust survivor Max Hyman bought the studio from Tommy Martin and renamed it The Palladium Dance Hall (Sanabria 2000). It became known as The Palladium Ballroom or El Palladium. The Puente show was so popular that Hyman made it a regular Sunday afternoon gig and opened the doors to all races. Middle-class blacks left the Apollo Theater and the Renaissance Ballroom to dance downtown. In the 1950s and early 1960s, a generation of Latinos came from Jimmy's Bronx Café, La Conga, or China Doll to hear the music and dance.

Thus, the club was famous for bringing together celebrities, artists, and people of all colors and persuasions to hear the Latin beats. It set the stage for the disco era ideal of races comingling on the dance floor.

At El Palladium, New York Latino dance culture fed into disco. The great uptown dancers did the Mambo there. The teenage children they brought along developed the Hustle, for dancing to disco music. In the 1970s, those kids were invited to discos everywhere to inspire and teach by example.

The second-floor El Palladium was at Fifty-third Street and Broadway. On Wednesdays, Fridays, Saturdays, and Sundays the three great Latin bandleaders Tito Rodriguez, Tito Puente, and Machito, tried to outdo each other. They challenged dancers with differing accented beats. A Wednesday night dance contest was popular. Everyone dressed to go downtown. Early birds paid 50 cents and those arriving later paid 2 dollars for entrance. The club closed at 4 a.m.

Floor shows featured professionals in mambo acts: Augie and Margo Rodriguez, Joe Vega, Michael "Mike" Terrace nee Guitterez and Elita, and wild woman from the Catskills Tybee Afra. They were paid 15 dollars a week. Celebrities came for the Wednesday night dance lesson. At this top Latin night spot, one could spot the likes of Marlon Brando, or "witness the sordid drama of hustling and drug dealing" that followed club culture into the 1990s and beyond (Settimelli 2007).

When El Palladium closed in 1966, Roseland was the place to dance the Hustle or The Chez José in the Upper West Side Park Plaza Hotel (Salazar 2000). That year, also at Broadway and Fifty-third Street, the new large-scale, multimedia Cheetah opened and in its four-year life there, 1970s disco was born of 1960s go-go. The phenomena would metastasize and live on, for better or worse, as the disco era.

The Limelight

A Limelight existed at 91 Seventh Avenue South just below Christopher Street from 1973 to 1980. That Latino, underground club is remembered, on the Web site disco-disco.com, as the first gay bar to admit women.

In 1984, a Limelight opened in a fortress-like corner church in Chelsea. In the late 1980s, Chelsea clubs served as after-opening watering holes for artists and their opening reception guests. Themed parties at the Limelight, The Tunnel, Danceteria, Pyramid, Mudd Club, and Area then featured one-night, salon-style art exhibits or themed art décor and a performance element. The guests were the performers. In the 1990s, party host Michael Alig threw a weekly Wednesday night "Disco

Limelight Disco, 1984. (Associated Press)

2000" in the rather spooky looking gothic-style stone church on the corner of Twentieth Street and Sixth Avenue. Alig, club kids, and their squashed futuristic aspirations are the subject of James St. James' book and the subsequent movie *Party Monster*. In summary, drug cocktails, cross-dressing, and fun-making, with an increasingly violent slant, resulted in the brutal murder of Angel Menendez. Menendez was a drug dealer whose clubbing costume was a large pair of wings. Alig is serving a 15-year prison sentence at this writing.

This eastern border of Chelsea was then a manufacturing area. As manufacturing in the city declined, and the garment industry moved to Far Eastern countries like the Philippines where labor was cheaper, Chelsea began to gentrify. Artists priced out of lofts farther south in

SoHo found expansive square footage in Chelsea's abandoned factories for living and working. However, it was desolate after working hours. Nightspots proliferated throughout this area that stretched west to the Hudson, north to Hell's Kitchen and Midtown, and south to the West Village.

The city-wide closing of psychiatric institutions around 1980 made the streets a destination for former inmates not quite ready for release. They were homeless. A series of muggings, rapes, and murders kept many who did have homes, inside them. New low-profile clubs opened in Chelsea for artists, VIPs, and working-class gay and straight people of different races in the first decade of the twenty-first century. News of violence against young women leaving clubs in the quiet pre-dawn hours scared area residents and revelers.

The journalist-historian Peter Braunstein, who wrote the journal article "Disco," unfortunately was one of the era's drug-addled victims. At this writing, he lives in the Clinton Correctional Facility. He wrote "Disco" four years before his notorious troubles were set off by a break-up. He infamously set fires in an apartment hallway and dressed as a fireman in order to gain entrance to the apartment of a female coworker. He held her captive for 12 hours and sexually assaulted her.

DJ Nicky Siano survived a serious drug habit and became a drug counselor. He has recently come out of retirement to play. Carroll is playing parties from Montreal to Miami, clean and sober.

Bridge and Tunnel Traffic

Disco created a discourse between European and American cities before and after its 1970s heyday here. Dancers from Jewish and Italian-American working-class neighborhoods fueled the American disco scene. Second-generation immigrant communities in New Jersey, Brooklyn, and Queens formed what were known as "bridge and tunnel" crowds that populated certain discos. When Steve Silano of Clifton, New Jersey, saw *Saturday Night Fever*, he said, "Hey, that's us!" referring to himself and three buddies who spent their weekly paychecks on everything related to disco nights. Aside from working with his father, a licensed plumber, and then with his brother and sister-in-law who started an e-fashion business, he and his friends spent their down-time waxing their cars, molding their hair, and buying clothes at the mall for the weekend (or mid-week) night out. New outfits were needed every week. They went to the neighborhood Joey's on Allwood Avenue in Clifton in the late 1970s. The club operated until 2007 (Silano 2008).

The self-described "nicky norkers" or "guidos" were enamored of themselves. These were "Don't touch my hair" kinds of guys. It was all about being at the top or acting and looking like you were. One-night-stands with good-looking girls attested to their greatness. The girls had to look beautiful and be great dancers. They would admire the dressed-to-the-nines hunks eyeing them from the side and ask them for a dance. The boys did not hesitate to say no to a girl who did not appeal to them or did not dance well enough. Dancing was the outlet.

The bar was about 30 square feet, Silano remembers. There were lots of lights and mirrors all around. The mirrored floor was handy for looking up the girls' dresses. The group remained loyal Joey's regulars, setting aside a weekday for the Clifton club even after they graduated to weekend nights in the city.

There, the coming of age group liked the Red Parrot or Visage, where the formality matched their jacket-and-tie preparations. The West side Visage, at Forty-first Street between Tenth and Eleventh Avenue, was the bomb (number one). The teens tipped generously and were on a first-name basis with the bartender. They would also tip to reserve ample floor space for their dance, should they feel inclined. They would bring a flask of Sambuca to save on drink expenses and order concoctions like Iced Tea (alcoholic) or Alabama Slammers. Wary of women taking advantage of them, they never bought them drinks. They merely bopped on the side, sipping, checking out the girls, preening, and decorating the place. If this sounds like role reversal, the clubs allowed for this. No one called it gay.

This group never got too drunk to drive home, and they all lived to tell about it. They may have encountered illicit drugs, homosexuality, and crime, and wondered—but they did not dwell or act on it. "It was a happy time," said Silano. They were stars, and it was a state of mind. In the club they were at once untouchable and sensual dancers. This paradoxical combination would live on in later dance styles, most notably hip-hop.

Disco's defining film *Saturday Night Fever* made the Brooklyn club 2001 Odyssey a famous location. It was just one of the local dives until *New York Magazine* writer Nik Cohn and then *Saturday Night Fever* director John Badham imagined the possibilities. Then everything changed. Badham had a revolutionary lighted floor installed. Certainly it was not the first. Loie Fuller's patented use of a lighted platform, documented in 1896 (Albright 2007, 55), accentuated the effect of her dances in flowing costumes. For social disco dancing, the lighted floor was an innovation that Badham may have seen in another club, for example Jerome's in Queens. With the success of the film, a second life, more glamorous than the first, commenced for the Odyssey.

Cohn is the movie's original screenwriter who wrote the inspiring *New York Magazine* article "Tribal Rites of the New Saturday Night." Cohn set his story in this club, and although the introduction to the article states, "Everything described in this article is factual and was either witnessed by me or told to me directly by the people involved," Cohn admitted later to having based Vincent (the basis for Tony Manero) on a mod, working-class London boy. He had only recently arrived in Brooklyn and appeared at Odyssey with the Bronx dancer Tu Sweet.

People were disappointed to hear, on the twentieth anniversary of the film's release, that there was no Vincent-cum-Tony Manero. One writer equated the questionable substance of the story with the emptiness of the era itself (McDuff 1996). He complained that the illustrations were painted, as if this proved Cohn's lack of real-life empirical knowledge.

In any case, Cohn's description of the "Face"—the male, Italian-American Bay Ridge local, club dancer extraordinaire and his preparation and dancing ritual—corroborates with many subsequent accounts of the era collected in nostalgic blog entries. Indeed, the club regulars on the *Saturday Night Fever* set were watchdogs, vetting the movie's correct portrayal of them.

> To qualify as an Odyssey Face, an aspirant need only be Italian, between the ages of eighteen and twenty-one, with a minimum stock of six floral shirts, four pairs of tight trousers, two pairs of Gucci-style loafers, two pairs of platforms, either a pendant or a ring, and one item in gold. In addition, he must know how to dance, how to drive, how to handle himself in a fight. He must have respect, even reverence, for Facehood, and contempt for everything else. He must also be fluent in obscenity, offhand in sex. Most important of all, he must play tough. (Cohn 1976, 4)

> *Saturday Night Fever* reopened the case for disco, yet the resulting
> nostalgia for the era is colored by, indeed, sometimes created
> by, the movie images. Some discophiles objected when they could
> not relate to its typecasting. See the following chapters for much
> more on this important disco tribute.

The Cohn article focuses on youth's hard-working weeks and hard-
playing weekends. The universality of that cannot be argued. His
models were a London working-class kid, the black, Rockland County
disco dancer who took him to Odyssey, and some dancers he saw there.

The aggregate character he created, the hardware clerk-cum-disco
dancer, lived on as a stereotype, one that Cohn created in the fictional
Vincent. Vincent and Tony sync with Silano, the plumber's helper
from Belleville. The Cohn story humanized the Bridge and Tunnel or
BBQ crowd where he had found *echt* disco dance. "Kids of sixteen to
twenty, full of energy, urgency, hunger. All the things, in fact, that the
Manhattan circuit, in its smugness, has lost."

Sal Fichera, an exercise physiologist from Queens, was always into
the physical. In 1977, at age 15, he followed his older sister to the studio, New York Hustle, Inc., in Flushing and then followed her to the
local clubs. Rusty Nail on Queens Boulevard in Woodside did not take
IDs. He wore platform shoes with marshmallow heels, bell-bottoms, a
shiny sky blue or white shirt open to the navel (he was always very fit
looking), and a gold chain. Things changed around the time that *Saturday Night Fever* came out. "Before the movie there were dress codes . . .
you had to be dressed up." Boys wore dress pants and blazer jackets,
and the girls wore dresses. "Disco seemed like it was dying. After the
movie, mobs of people came to the clubs." Pre-*Fever*, the girls would
ask if he could hustle before they would agree to a dance. Unlike
Silano, Fichera always asked. He went to Elephas in Bayside. The club
had great dancers among the 17- to 21-year-old crowd and the best
sound system. DJ Paul Casella and Jimmy Yu worked there. Fichera
was serious about dancing but not deaf to conversation about someone the management did not like and who was beaten up.

Others remember having been there the night serial killer David
Berkowitz, a.k.a. Son of Sam, shot a couple parked outside the club
in June 1977. Owner Mike Morash instituted valet parking and told

the kids to stay away for their own safety after the murder. It closed shortly after that.

"I was just a quiet guy who just wanted to dance and have fun," Fichera told me. He was not much of a conversationalist, but he could manage, "Would you like to dance." Arriving at 10:30 p.m. or 11:00 p.m. to hustle, he and his sister would separate, and then hustle again just before closing time when they got kicked out. They went on the weekends unless the club advertised a weekday disco party. The bar was set about one-third into the large, rectangular, ground floor space. Beyond that there were two dance floors—a large, round wood floor for hustle dancing and a smaller one next to it for top hustle dancers. Then, later they combined the floors into one larger one (Fichera 2008).

Infinity

Sally Helgesen wrote about Infinity in her 1977 *Harper's* article "Disco." At three on the morning of her visit, there were about 2,000 people in the 653 Broadway discotheque near Bleeker Street. The floor-through was one city block long. Infinity opened in 1975 and had wall-to-wall mirrors. Helgesen's crowd wore freaky costumes and masks. If you did not have a dance partner, you need only look in the mirror, noted Helgesen who saw a uniform dress code that created kaleidoscopic "kindred shapes." Decorating the two bars were two neon phalluses. The disco ball had space-age neon rings suspended around it, and the columns too were decorated with neon hoops. The continuous, repetitive beat of the music synchronized the dancers on the floor who appeared stupefied by some sense of anticipation, as if something would be happening. Finally, on Valentine's Day, 1979, the club burned down. People who hated disco derisively called the fire "the disco inferno." Only the ornate cast iron columns remained, minus their encircling neon hoops.

By accounts on the Web site disco-disco.com, dress was casual at Infinity, to say the least. Women wore hot pants, tank tops, and heels. The men wore jeans, sneakers, and no shirts. Quaaludes, cocaine, and amyl nitrate were as plentiful as the free, fresh pears.

Infinity had some nudity, which is why Fichera wanted to go there. He described giant fruit salad bowls in the center, and he knew it was a drug marketplace. Girls would take their clothes off if they got hot, he said. On the mezzanine, people would have sex. Fichera might

Dancers with poppers at Infinity in 1975. (Photo by Allan Tannenbaum)

have liked to take part in that, but he was still shy at 21. The dancing was freestyle. Though he liked Hustle, he accepted the fact that there wasn't as much of that any more. Another draw at Infinity—they were open all night long. "I would step out at 5:30 in the morning."

The Hustle had peaked by the time *Saturday Night Fever* was released, and freestyle came back. Rockers crowded the discotheques

Infinity owner Maurice Brahms also owned a share in Underground, on Union Square. He had to sell after he was convicted of skimming profits from the club New York, New York in 1980. He stayed on and worked as a promoter for new owner Ronna Juliano. His wife Vivian owned Red Zone in Hell's Kitchen, the far, western patch of Midtown. The city cracked down on street noise after area residents organized in block associations to try and safeguard the neighborhood from violence. But Brahms said the Hell's Kitchen neighborhood held the threat of violence, and he sometimes feared for the club (Nieves 1990). Indeed, it could be argued that discos were bastions of safety, with their heavily guarded entrances and hospitable atmosphere. In the comfort and safety of a chosen family, dancers enjoyed uninhibited fun.

Sal's Hustle Playlist:

"If There's Love": USA-European Connection

"From Here To Eternity": Giorgio Moroder

"That's The Way I Like It": KC & the Sunshine Band

"I'm Your Boogie Man": Tavares

"Heaven Must Be Missing An Angel": Donna Summer

"I Will Survive": Gloria Gaynor

with people in casual, nice jeans. Fichera went to the more upscale, mid-town Xenon then.

From 1978 to 1984, Xenon disco operated in the 1918 neo-Georgian Henry Miller theater at 24 West Forty-third Street. In the early 1970s, male porno films were shown there. During its life as Xenon, in May 1983, Terrence McNally's comedy *The Ritz* was played with Holly Woodlawn (of Warhol fame) and Casey Donovan, a gay porn star. A ticket to the show included dancing after curtain (Bloom 2004).

Farther east, Fichera frequented Townhouse 48 between Third and Second Avenues, where Fridays were for singles and Saturdays were for dating, in 1978 and 1979. The club had cushions on the top floor and dancing underneath.

Fichera would spend an extra $5 to see top entertainers at Long Island clubs. In 1982, he saw Madonna sing "Starlite, Starbright" at Uncle Sam's in Hempstead.

Gloria Gaynor performed "I Will Survive" in 1978 at Cherry's in Glen Cove. Around 1976 Thelma Houston sang "Don't Leave Me This Way" with Ecstasy, Passion & Pain at Jerome's on Queens Boulevard. "If the [hustle] dancing wasn't up to par, then it didn't matter who the DJ was . . . I just wanted to see good dancers. I was looking to learn and be inspired. Once I got into the dancing I felt like I was just floating on air." Prior to *Fever*, everyone hustled. After it, Fichera saw line dances and freestyles in the Queens discos.

"Brooklyn dancers were cool. You just wanted to experience that. Apparently, Italian-Americans from Brooklyn were quite different from Italian Americans from Queens. They were sharp. They looked good but they were tough. They liked to fight. I was with my sister and I bumped one of them and he shoved me across the floor. I was surrounded by about fifteen guys." As an outsider Fichera was turned off by the aggressiveness. He went to 2001 Odyssey and did not particularly like it. It was tiny. But he *was* impressed with the Brooklyn crowd after all. "In Brooklyn, even young girls (we called them 'mini-guidos') were sharply dressed even at twelve years old. I was fascinated by that even though I initially had some problems."

Queens clubs were much bigger and more open. Lemon Tree was a small restaurant and popular dance club on Austin Street in Forest Hills. After 10 p.m. the tables in back would be cleared for dancing. Between 1977 and 1982 Fichera went with friends from that neighborhood and found a nice crowd, great music, and attractive women. After Elephas, Environs on Bell Boulevard in Bayside was the place to go. The small, basement club had fantastic music and good hustle dancers among the Brooklyn, Queens, and Long Island crowd.

At St. Johns University in Brooklyn, in the last years of the 1970s, Fichera started a Wednesday afternoon dance club in the Rathskeller lounge. It had vending machines, a refreshment counter, and folding tables. A mobile DJ came in. Although the club had 20 to 25 members, 50 to 80 showed up to dance between classes. It was truly multicultural, and that's where he made his peace with "the cuisines" (Brooklyn Italian-American cousins).

But Fichera noticed another rift. Revelers would be waiting in line to go into a club, and people would yell out their car windows, "Disco Sucks!" At the street-level Rathskeller, someone threw a bottle of acid through the window onto the dance floor. One night in 1974 or 1975, Fichera and his friends mistakenly ended up at a Long Island Rum Bottom on a rock night. "One guy leaned over and said, 'you guys don't belong here.' The distinction was clear. I wore polyester pants. I was clean-shaven. I had a 'dry d.a.,' blow-dried. They had long hair and dungarees." It was time for a quick exit.

He was 25, graduating, and engaged to be married. Tuesday was the night for hustle dancing at La Shea near Shea Stadium, in Queens. There were many Latinos there, and he met a dance partner, who would lead, teaching him steps.

Fichera started dancing at clubs in Manhattan like Le Farfalle where all the best dancers from outside and inside the city (of Manhattan) converged. It was touted as the most beautiful and expensively appointed club and had waterfalls and state-of-the-art lighting, according to Boodikka, at discomusic.com, but its glory was short-lived. Across from the famous Roseland, the best Latino dancers were at Ipanema, where the men would hustle together if there were no women available. They could lead and follow, and Fichera learned the steps by watching them. Gay Latinos at Ipanema were discreet about their sexuality. There were drugs, but that did not interest Fichera because he had always lived a healthy lifestyle.

Reflections

In 1976, Billy Carroll was house DJ four nights a week for the popular club called Down Under, where straight blacks danced. Friday and Saturday nights, admittance was for members. Whites and Latinos went to the nearby Copacabana except on Sunday night, which was for blacks. They shared the same owner and managed to avoid competing for particular patrons. One night there was a drug-related shooting at Down Under. Everyone panicked, including Carroll, who has since buried this deep in the recesses of his memory. He ran for the door, unwittingly leading the way. He knew the fire exits and had the wherewithal to flip on all the lights as he left. Three people died. Carroll and the disco ultimately survived the traumatic experience.

The club reopened as Reflections, and people danced on. The new format was after-work parties on Thursdays and Friday nights. Carroll worked from about 5 p.m. to 5 a.m. for another nine years and may have seen Sal Fichera on the dance floor. Fichera went to Xenon and Reflections in the late 1980s.

In the 1990s, Fichera moved into the city. He was single and going out dancing. He frequented Cheetah Lounge on Thirteenth Street, where he met his wife. He also went to Palladium on Fourteenth Street. He liked the outstanding atmosphere and sound system. Club goers danced in a performing area lit by theater lights.

When Palladium opened, Billy Carroll was awed by its spectacular interior, a replica of the *Saturday Night Fever* set. Carroll was then working again at the gay parties at Men's Club and Boy's Club for the younger crowd at the Building. The dances were "lemming-like," he said. It was a place where the East Village boys with shaved heads and tattoos, and alternative lifestyle, met the uniformed, built, shirtless Chelsea males. The Ritz popped up in the historic East Village Webster Hall in the 1980s as a rock club. In the 1990s, it was called

Webster Hall again, and Fichera, from another world altogether, went dancing there on Thursday nights. Mondays or weekend nights he was at the China Club on the East Side. The 20-year hustle veteran was also dancing at the small bar Juke Box in the Kips Bay Area and at Copacabana on disco night, west of the theater district.

Seventies nightlife was a netherworld where people of different walks of life, social and economic status, skin color, and pasts met. Some clubs were segregated, with black, gay, white, straight, Latinos congregating in different places by design or choice, but more and more clubs brought people together. In the disco ideal, if you could dance, the color of your skin or your sexual preference did not matter. The discotheque was potentially a great equalizer where "celebrated" and "marginalized" were meaningless.

Grand Ballroom

Nuyoricans (the generation of New Yorkers born of Puerto Rican parents) and young Latinos in Spanish Harlem, Inwood, and the South Bronx watched their parents' Mambo and updated the steps to go with the new disco music. They wowed downtown kids, and ultimately, dancers around the world, with a new dance. In the South Bronx, Latina girls were creating new touch-dancing steps while the boys did high rock, a battle dance. 310 ½ in the Bronx and Footsteps on the Lower Eastside would let the kids in with their freestyle and high rock. In 1973 the boys, including Hustle legend William "Billy" Fajardo, took interest in the girls' new dance at the Forty-fifth Street Grand Ballroom. They honed their skills and competed at the midtown Latino clubs. They danced at Cheetah, according to Izzy Sanabria, publisher of *Latin NY* magazine, established in 1973. Manhattan's Upper Eastside Barney Google's and the Corso played disco music in the breaks between band sets. Hustle followed.

Roseland

Roseland Ballroom dates from before the Depression. Big bands played for whites only. In the 1960s, founder Louis Brecker famously banned the twist in favor of cheek-to-cheek dancing, but his daughter Nancy took over operations and set up a disco night to bring young people in. The room, which she had decorated, filled to capacity. Male and female taxi dancers, semi-pros, danced with customers at $1 per dance. People came to do the hustle on the magnificent dance floor in the late 1970s when Olga Varvaro gave one-hour hustle lessons from the stage. "Roselanders are now into the hustle," she said. Latin and American bands alternated every half hour on hustle nights. "Today's Hustle is the only new dance suitable for ballroom dancing since the Cha-Cha in the late Fifties," said Don De Natale who called himself the "Prince of Roseland" (Judge 1981). He plays the Emcee in the 1977 James Ivory movie *Roseland*, which shows hustle dancing at its very best. The dance scene in Spike Lee's *Malcolm X* is filmed at the club. In 1984, a Staten Island teen was shot and killed on the dance floor, and disco night was dropped. Roseland then hosted rock concerts and special events.

Once a month at Roseland, in 2008, Felix Hernandez's Rhythm Revue held a giant electric slide at 1 a.m., after which disco reigned. He spun "Shame" and "I Will Survive" for the crowd. The Revue party sold out 3,000 or more $20 tickets on a typical Saturday night. Fernandez started the Revue on WBGO radio, the noncommercial National Public Radio jazz station in 1986, and tied it to the monthly Roseland party.

Disco-era dances live on around the world. A (geographically) scattered community of professional dancers and social dancers do the hustle. Many night people came to shun the word "disco" and the mention of circuit parties because of their associations with drugs and AIDS, but they did not stop going out to clubs where layers of sampled tracks create a fabric of sound. Pop-up parties, the Loft, discos, dressing up to reinvent oneself for the night, hustle and freestyle dancing to recorded music are certainly alive and well at this writing.

Beneath the smooth exterior, the criminal underworld had a hand in club ownership and protection of the earliest West Village clubs. $2,000 a month would keep the NYPD away from the doors of gay clubs like the Saint or the Sanctuary (Lawrence 2003). In the twenty-first century, the word "underground" is outdated. Nostalgia for the disco era means remembering that shortened lives and unfulfilled dreams forestalled the Love, Peace, and Harmony. Dancer's sweat best generated the heavenly disco aura.

2

Wild West (of New York City)

A group of club entrepreneurs bought an abandoned soap factory in Palisades Park, New Jersey, and transformed it into a spot for dancing fun. They kept the soap bubbles and hung a small Cessna airplane from the ceiling for décor. Colored chase lights flashed under the dance floor where dancers did the Bus Stop or Continental Walk. Free dancing and Hustle happened on a separate platform. Top disco stars performed, including the Trammps, Gloria Gaynor, Donna Summer, Archie Bell and the Drells, and Evelyn King. Former club visitors commenting on the Web site disco-disco.com saw local celebrities like John Travolta there. They remembered former Soap Factory DJs Alan Grohkle and Lou Capurso, who also posted on the site. DJ Bobby Guttadero worked there, according to NYTimes.com. On Sundays, Soap Factory hosted a teen club, where Capurso played top 40 pop songs. After disco's heyday, the owners changed the music to rock in hopes of attracting college crowds. The day that disco died at Soap Factory, Ayatollah Khomeini had just taken Americans hostage. The Twisted Sisters were singing "The Ayatollah Sucks." Patrons started ripping down and burning the disco posters. While rock raged upstairs, downstairs continued as a disco for a time with disco sets and the hanging airplane (discomusic.com n.d.). From 1977 to 1979, the club was the location of the TV dance show *Soap Factory* (see p. 142).

Philadelphia and Westerly

"Philly soul" made Philadelphia a source of disco, and it was on the map as an urban disco center early on. Radio DJ Ron Joseph, doing business as RJ, opened the first Philadelphia disco in 1966, an under 21 dance club on the University of Pennsylvania campus. The following year, he opened Groove at Broad and Locust where his WIFI FM radio show was live. A visit to Arthur's in New York City had inspired him. RJ played Gloria Gaynor's "Honey Bee" and "When Will I See You Again" by The Three Degrees. He created several television shows including *RJ & Company*, a teen disco on Channel 29. It syndicated around the country as *Disco USA* in 1975 (The Broadcast Pioneers of Philadelphia n.d.). A Wildwood, New Jersey, beach was one location for his televised dance parties.

Joseph was a teenage dancer on *American Bandstand* in the 1960s. "A lot of the songs had a dance beat back then." Kids watching on Saturday morning were inspired, even if subliminally. Looking back on those times, Joseph lamented the changes on the dance floor. "Disco had class and finesse . . . they had to dress up, that's why it died. Today they just want to be themselves." Dancers would put on costumes and become stars. It was fun, warm, and fuzzy; and it was healthy the way the kids were dancing with their whole bodies (Joseph ca.2000).

Meanwhile, another Philadelphia radio DJ started out as a bandstand dancer. Jerry Blavat was emceeing teen dances in 1966 at Chez Vous. Blavat is best known for his allegiance to doo-wop and oldies, but he did catch disco fever when in 1979 he started taping the teen *Discophonic Scene* in the Cherry Hill, NJ Winner's Circle disco. The show was notably mixed-race. Amateur dancing alternated with musical spots by Gloria Gaynor, Karen Young, Patti LaBelle, First Choice, and other stars. Blavat named himself "The Geater with the Heater," and a Billboard writer described how "he moves along and chats with dancers in his inimitable, hip fashion" (Orodenker 1979).

Cleveland has a disco heritage and a disco page in its Rock 'n' Roll Hall of Fame Web site. While in many cases, after its fall from grace, disco was erased from memory and history, every urban center has its disco story. In particular, Twin Cities DJ Ronny D, a.k.a. Ronald Ramsdell, exemplifies disco lovers' loyalty.

Disco spread quickly to Italian-American communities in Minneapolis. Black communities there fed into the Twin Cities disco phenomenon, as they did in Chicago and Cleveland, where rock, R&B, soul, and jazz flourished.

Minneapolis DJ Ronny D went to New York for the love of disco and brought new inspiration to his radio show and club performances. An upscale crowd listened to his music at Scottie's on 7th in the mid-1970s. It opened in a deco-era movie house. One patron commenting on the Web site discomusic.com told of returning night after night to dance to "Devil's Gun" by CJ&Co. Another called it "the Studio 54 of Minneapolis." The two-year-old club closed down in July 1976 to make way for a shopping mall.

First Avenue & 7th St. Entry is a rock 'n' roll club with some disco history. It was a Greyhound bus depot in 1937. The building underwent its first nightclub incarnation in 1968, emerging as The Depot. Joe Cocker performed the inaugural show. Steve McClellan and Jack Meyers took over and the club, in the last years of the 1970s, was discofied as an Uncle Sam's franchise. ChuckB on the Web site discomusic.com described it as strictly disco. The Village People played in 1979. Minneapolis native and singer/songwriter Neil Conrad remembers the pick-up group Lips, Inc., premiering "Funkytown" at the club.

Under McClellan, Uncle Sam's became Sam's and again featured live rock bands. The disco dancers cleared the floor, and the club hosted a Dump Disco weekend. Meanwhile, Uncle Sam's would thrive nationally in party towns like Troy, Buffalo, Levittown, and South Beach.

On New Year's day of 1981, Sam's took the name First Avenue. It sported a purple, plush covered stage and attracted the beautiful people. It catered to dancers with contests. Yet, its day as the discotheque Uncle Sam's is left unsung on the club's Web site, where it is branded as a rock club. Its rock club's history lives on in the 1984 Prince movie *Purple Rain*. The owners, however, were not solely responsible for the trend. The polarization of black and white communities ruled the changing music and dance genres featured in Twin Cities' clubs. In the 1970s, they were either black or white. Disco's rainbow ethic did not support long-held prejudice that favored segregation.

Minneapolis disco dancers remember a Firecracker drink. By the late 1970s, in Minneapolis and nearby St. Paul, one could choose between disco, punk, new wave, and rock. In the 1990s, First Avenue hosted hip-hop and in the new century, dance, electronica, and techno. Meanwhile, Scandinavian immigrants popularized folk and ballroom dances like the Waltz and Polka. In 2009, First Avenue Mainroom had a Saturday night dance event featuring a mix of music including classic disco.

DJ Ronny D continues his radio show and mobile gigs, championing reigning disco stars like Donna Summer, whom he interviewed on KFAI before the release of her 2008 *Crayons*. Ronny played classic disco New Year's Eve, 2009, at the one-year-old Seven Sushi Ultralounge at Seventh and Hennepin, in the heart of the nightclub district.

The World's Largest Disco

In Buffalo, a Western New York college and working-class town that borders Lake Erie, young people caught on to disco as they did in more populous urban centers. Marty Angelo helped organize The World's Largest Disco at the Buffalo Convention Center in 1979, drawing a crowd of 13,000. The *Guinness Book of World Records* listed it as the largest disco event of all time.

Angelo was very involved with the Buffalo disco community. He had finished taping the TV show *Disco Step-by-Step*, which was set in Buffalo Area discos. The show was still airing at the time of the World's Largest Disco. It featured 10-minute lessons by professional instructors from local studios (see pp. 144–145). Angelo was also coordinator of the Disco Spinners and president of the Buffalo Record Pool.

Local TV and radio stations sponsored the World's Largest Disco, primarily. Gloria Gaynor and the Trammps highlighted shows by local and national DJs, including New York City's Bobby Guttadero. The event featured an International Disco Dance Championship, a bar, food, and clothing concessions.

On its fifteenth anniversary, the party resumed as a charity fundraising event, with Angelo's blessing. Since then, it happens annually, and to date, it has raised over $2 million for various charities.

John Ceglia's wife, a professional dancer and instructor, taught him the disco steps. Every weekend, he and his friends went to the club Fridays and Saturdays. In 1978, he was a senior in high school. He had been practicing with his friend's turntables. He asked Leonard Casola, owner of Sgt. Pepper's, for a job. He started that weekend at $20 a night. He then worked at the 747 Club. Ceglia took the 400-mile trip into New York that summer and was "blown away by the mastery the DJ had over the people," he told Bernard Lopez of discomusic.com. Ceglia went on to become a respected and expert DJ at the New York City clubs

Underground, The River Club, and Studio 54. He liked the diversity of the City club experience and went to the Garage and elsewhere to hear different DJ styles. Club goers remember him as the Ice Palace DJ on Fire Island. He also worked at the Fire Island Pavilion. Ceglia wanted to work where the people were most receptive to the music. At Pavilion, he made a connection with a recording studio where he trained as an engineer. Ceglia quit DJ work in the mid-1980s and went back home to Buffalo in the early 1990s. He made his comeback at "The World's Largest Disco."

San Francisco

Among pre-Stonewall bars, necessarily underground, the mood at The Rendezvous, a gay bar with an unmarked door on Sutter, was very repressed, according to Joshua Gamson, biographer of the San Francisco-based musician and performer Sylvester (Gamson 2005, 48). The Rendezvous clientele, largely gay workers in the financial district around Castro and Market Streets, liked listening to Barbra Streisand. The Black Cat Café was an important gay nightspot on Montgomery Street, where Allen Ginsberg and other beats, poets, and sailors gathered. The owner fought in Supreme Court when the state suspended his liquor license. The court decided that it was not illegal to serve homosexuals, but an amendment allowed continuing raids and shuttering of gay establishments. The Black Cat closed with a final Halloween party (juice and soda were sold at the bar) in 1963. Then, a 1964 *Life* magazine article drew gay men and lesbians to San Francisco and helped establish it as the gay capital. The Black Cat lives on as The Bohemian Bar in Jack Kerouac's *On the Road* and as an emblem of gay rights (Sparkletack 2008).

Meanwhile, Sylvester was a teen growing up in the South Central, Watts Area of Los Angeles. He liked to "fish" or pass as a woman. He went out with his friends dressed in homemade costumes— sequined platform shoes or roller skates, a Twiggy wig, skirts, and dresses. He and his friends went to clubs for African Americans: the Clowns, the Hyde Park, the Belmont, and Bucket of Blood. The only club for gay blacks was Horseshoe (Gamson, 33). Black power was rising, and the city was reeling from the 1965 Watts riots. In six days, 261 buildings burned and 34 people had died. In the looting that followed, Sylvester grabbed wigs, hairspray, and lipsticks. He formed a performing group called The Disquotays.

Sylvester's is a story of the way in which disco helped heal the world. In 1969, he graduated from Jordan High School at age 21. He made off to San Francisco, and there he developed a devoted following. He was the West Coast embodiment of disco, combining attributes of gay men and 1970s soul sisters, in performances that "exploded in a torrent of sensuality" (Gamson, 111).

In the early 1970s, after Stonewall, newly liberated gays flocked to San Francisco. Carl Whitman, in his 1972 *Gay Manifesto,* called the city a gay refugee camp. Hippie Haight-Ashbury had spawned free love, and the city was congenial for jubilant gays. Many bars sprang up in the North Beach Area. The Mineshaft, the Shed on Market Street, Cabaret, Silver Dollar, The Purple Onion, and Manas were popular. Fancier choices were Chez Jacques, Sutters Mill, and hotel bars. Uncle Donald's Web site names the City Dump and Scott's Pit, a lesbian bar.

When Sylvester arrived in the city, he met like-minded people at the Capri or the Stud bar. Castro Street and The Castro neighborhood became the West Coast equivalent of New York's Christopher Street and West Village. Locals called their activist Harvey Milk "The Mayor." Then he did become the first openly gay public official. Sylvester also took the soapbox, performing on a small, outdoor stage

Sylvester. (Photofest)

When asked about heroes, Sylvester is first on the lips of gay men who went out dancing in the 1970s. "Sylvester embodied the disco fantasy in which race and gender lose their relevance..." (Gamson 2008, 3). However, Sylvester's celebratory music was the voice of gay pride. In bars, clubs, and concert halls, Martha Wash and Izora Rhodes, as Two Tons o' Fun, backed him. After a historical, sold-out Sylvester concert at the War Memorial Opera House on March 11, 1979, Mayor Diane Feinstein declared it "Sylvester Day" and presented him with the keys to the city. Everyone sang along to his ballad "You Make Me Feel (Mighty Real)." Two months later, on May 21, a "White Night" demonstration protested Supervisor Dan White's mild five-to-seven-year sentence for killing Supervisor Harvey Milk and San Francisco Mayor George Moscone. Sylvester's voice helped foster that fight (see pp. 83–84).

at The Castro's open-air street fairs. Dance culture was strong. Expression through dance was everywhere because gay men and lesbians were suppressed for so long. San Francisco's growing gay community was breaking out.

Most people consider Toad Hall The Castro's first dance bar. Opened in 1971, it was ahead of the crowd in abandoning the jukebox for taped music. Then it was one of the first to hire a DJ. Before Toad, gays had been meeting in seedy dive bars. "Toad Hall welcomed us with a warm friendly smile into a clean, well-decorated establishment," says Uncle Donald (Donald 1998). The club took the name of the misfit toad's home in the classic *Wind and the Willow*. A group of four proprietors opened it, including Ron Estes and David Monroe, owners of popular, nearby Lion Pub. They brought over that club's longhaired Stan Walker to manage Toad. The club survived three fires, one started by rows of votive candles that served as décor and atmospheric lighting. The cleanups were community efforts and occasions for even more celebration.

In Armistead Maupin's serial in the *San Francisco Chronicle* and later collected in three books, the free-spirited residents of a rooming house meet at the EndUp. Maupin chose this club for his tome about San Francisco life. As he revisualized the scene in a 1994 miniseries, the freestyle dancers wore casual sports attire or swirly, silky dresses. Maupin's writing spoofed the bizarre sex and drug bazaar, as seen through the eyes of a Cleveland–born-and-bred newcomer character.

Al Hanken opened the (real) EndUp in 1973. He "lived the swinging 1970s lifestyle to the fullest" (English 2003). The club was suffering from mismanagement, drug addiction, and the AIDS crisis by the mid-1980s but celebrated its thirtieth anniversary in 2006. It managed to ride the various waves of sexual revolutions by diversifying. It had a low-frills charm that its owners maintained, along with its inclusivity. Hanken died of AIDS, and his brothers kept the club afloat, despite periodic police threats of shutdown. "I loved it because everyone was welcome there. Everyone was there to have a good time and dance to great music. It didn't matter whether you were gay or straight or black or white or whatever," said long-time patron Sydney Leung who bought the club in the 1990s (Picture 2006). Gay and straight nights alternated. Music and dance styles alternated too. Sam Whiting in a 1994 *Chronicle* article called the club a San Francisco phenomenon, citing a "mysterious energy" in its marathon, round-the-clock dancing and resting ritual and the changing of the crowd's sexual orientation from afternoon to evening to morning (Whiting 2006).

Twenty-two-year-old gay DJ Johnny "Disco" Hedges worked at the Mineshaft, then the Cabaret and City Disco. He started the record label Megatone and produced Sylvester and others. Hedges learned from Jim Burgess at New York's 12 West. Hedges also started the San Francisco record pool BAADA. DJ Tim Rivers worked at Mineshaft and Bones and then I-Beam. He contracted HIV and died at age 45 in 1995. Both Hedges and Rivers received Billboard awards (S. Shapiro 2006).

By the mid-1970s, San Francisco was a homeland for gay men and lesbians. The Cabaret became the enormous City Disco. I-Beam, Trocadero Transfer, and Dreamland were the large discos in the later part of the decade. People tripped on acid for extended energy and deeper experience of the sensual environment. Dick Collier's Trocadero Transfer, a.k.a. the Troc, opened in 1977 at 520 Fourth Street and closed in 1983. It had a state-of-the-art Graebar sound system like the Saint's and a sprung wood floor for the dancers' optimum comfort. DJ Bobby Viteritti took over from Gary Tighe in late 1977 and worked from 11 p.m. to 8 a.m. The crowd averaged 1,000 predominantly gay patrons but included some straight, hard-core dancers—those who were still up in the wee hours. At 4 a.m. when a new, after-hours crowd appeared,

Trocadero workers (left, Bobby Viteritti; center, Billy Langenheim) at a San Francisco Pride parade. (Bobby Viteritti)

he would ramp up. Gina Spirsch would spread wax powder on the dance floor, and the dancers would continue through sunup. When the light came in through the six skylights, six volunteers climbed onto the roof and pulled tarps over the glass for an encore set.

The Troc did not have alcohol for most of its years. The experience was drug based. In its later years, it did serve alcohol and admitted more women. The right drugs, dances, DJ, time, and place made late 1978–1981 the golden years at Troc when Viteritti "brought a whole new feeling and meaning to the dance," said Paul Parker in David Diebold's definitive book *Tribal Rites*. It was a bizarre, late-night place with a lot of drugs, tripping, and poppers. Until 10 a.m., Billy Langenheim and Viteritti controlled the consciousness. Michael Whitehead called the atmosphere "complete euphoria—both physically and mentally." The women who went wanted the challenge. There was an initiation process where the family of dancers on the floor would teach newcomers how to party properly. It was inappropriate to have just one partner, said Theresa Mahar, "You would get out there and literally dance with everybody" (Diebold 1986, 130).

The matchbook covers boasted, "The ultimate in space, light and sound," and partygoers agreed this was an accurate description. In 1982, the club declined as the music shifted to hard rock and punk. An incident where Collier fired the entire staff also set its downturn. The new fad, disco, exemplified in *Saturday Night Fever*, the Bee Gees, and TV dance moves, was not at all recognizable to the Thursday-to-Sunday Troc dance family.

Viteritti moved to Dreamland when that club offered more money. Troc dancers followed, but the new location, with its white walls, was just not the same. It was comparable to Flamingo, with a more professional crowd "standing and posing but never really perspiring." Dreamland and Music Hall were for "a different kind of gay man." You could wear what you wanted to at the Troc.

Viteritti started to burn out around 1981. He had brought a level of artistry to the craft of changing records. He also set standards for professional wages. In 2007, a pearl-themed, pop-up "Remember the Party" celebration happened in the original Troc space. Decades later, where New Yorkers are remembering the party, Viteritti is there (see pp. 81–83).

In one of the extra-large venues, the mega-party Night Flight featured acrobats, a talking robot, and an orgy room. Night Flight continues as a more-or-less annual party, with people jetting thousands of miles to attend. Trippin' on the Moon, Saint-at-Large, and Holy Spirit Dance Club are Saint reunions. Halloween Black and Easter White events continue from the very first circuit parties in New York.

The stereotypical West is more American, *more* open, bigger, and wilder. San Francisco's mega-parties started popping up outside of the regular venues when straight, mainstream disco infiltrated the original clubs. Gay people still wanted to go out dancing, of course. At one party held at Kabuki, leather men tap-danced out of dry ice fog and 24 Japanese schoolgirls did a fan dance on a raised, central platform. Then the release of the Village People's "San Francisco" song was cause célèbre at Kabuki. An array of speakers blasted it from overhead. In 1978, A Salute to the Men of San Francisco was held at the Galleria Design Center. Sylvester's appearance was an attraction. Troc owner Dick Collier used the gigantic Cow's Palace for a King Tut extravaganza. The party was a camp, celebratory emanation of the touring Treasures of Tutankhamen exhibit. This wondrous and wildly popular show stopped in San Francisco and New York where the

Paradise Garage's Tut Tut Tut party riffed off the new, blockbuster-museum-show phenomenon. But Collier had to change the date several times because of trouble with the city. With all the confusion, only 200 complimentary ticketed guests showed up to see elephants, lions, and more from the theme park Marine World Africa USA step out from a giant Pyramid. Hollywood movie sets were a handy source for mega-party décor. In The Mothership party that David Bandy threw in an L.A. observatory, a spaceship descended from a helicopter over the dance floor.

Diebold, the San Francisco music producer who chronicled gay club life, boasted that San Francisco dancers are serious about the ritual of coming together to dance. By comparison, he decried Sanctuary in New York as a site for "black mass rituals" and "orgiastic congregation." He called the San Francisco club Dreamland "pristine, clean, and even conservative." The balconies at the Troc were for sitting and viewing the dance floor and not for sex, as they were in New York's Saint, he said. Diebold was obviously proud of the San Francisco life.

Dancers also remember Ruby Skye, DV8, Pleasuredome, Powerhouse, Detour, 1015, and Arena (White Light Productions 2009). They attended Tea Dances with DJ Michael Garrett at I-Beam. Tea Dances became a safer alternative to the drugs and sex associated with all-night clubbing. City Disco was a restaurant, disco, showroom, and stores. It was the early stomping ground for producer and disco entrepreneur Marty Blecman, Hedges, disco music maker Patrick Cowley, and Sylvester. By 1978, it was becoming less and less cool. Gays abandoned it for the newer, bigger, above-mentioned clubs. Said legendary Troc DJ Viteritti, "The queens were calling it 'disco' for a long time . . . the word didn't leave a bad taste in your mouth [then]" (Diebold, 156). Consider Sylvester's teen group, the Disquotays, formed in the late 1960s.

Spreading the Love

Dancer Karen Lustgarten went to San Francisco's Twin Peaks neighborhood, to the small clubs and dance bars around Market and Castro Streets, already a gay capital in 1973. In the mixed-race crowd, she saw "restless natives" dancing freestyle steps that reflected the new fluid, orchestral-backed songs by Gloria Gaynor or Tavares. Lustgarten broke down the dance style and started teaching people in her basement. The demand grew and she sought a bigger venue. She met Stu Goldberg who had just opened a large disco on the corner of Columbus and Lombard, called Dance Your Ass Off. The enormous two-story DYAO, formerly the elite, gay Olympus nightclub, catered to a straight crowd in 1977. Goldberg said that for the previous 10 years, discos had been confined to San Francisco's gay community. Admission was $1 Monday and Tuesday and $2 Wednesday through Sunday (R. Williams 1995). Goldberg allowed her to bring several hundred students for lessons before the club opened. Lustgarten collaborated with club DJ Marc Richardson on the lesson plan and flashed hand-signal directions to him in the upstairs booth. Richardson did the lights too. Her *révérence*, or closing instruction, was "The club is now open. You can stay and dance." Everyone would enter the celebratory atmosphere of the bar, party lights, and hours of music and dance.

Lustgarten's lessons moved to the nearby City Disco after she and Goldberg had a disagreement over the rights to her invented technique. Pete Struve, another mid-1970s DYAO DJ, recalled a crowd of 1,400. Struve was light man and maintained the technical equipment in addition to working at the turntables. He broke the song "Giddyap Girl" (by the Bareback Rockers) in the Bay Area.

"Shame, Shame, Shame/Spirit of the Boogie," "Think About It" (Lynn Collins), "You're The One" (The Three Degrees), and "Fight The Power" (The Isley Brothers) were Struve's anthems. Like a radio DJ, he would introduce the songs, especially less-familiar ones. He had gone to the Bailey School of Broadcasting and aspired to be an FM DJ. He made $30, four nights a week at the club. Struve controlled the décor from his booth, where he could engage five mirrored balls, a strobe, and a laser-beam projector. He and Lustgarten enjoyed the spectacle of all the bell-bottom clad dancers on the floor doing the L.A. Hustle, a line Hustle (Robertson 1976).

Lustgarten admitted noticing amyl nitrate or poppers at City Disco, but otherwise she was largely oblivious to any drug use. She and her students were there to dance. Goldberg estimated that 60 percent of the patrons were gay at the City. Both City and DYAO had two floors, room for 800 dancers, and expensive fixtures and equipment. They were San Francisco's two largest discos. City had a "computerized light show" (R. Williams 1995).

Disco spread to urban areas around the country. In 1979, in residential neighborhoods around the San Fernando Valley, mobile DJs were masters of ceremonies at parties in roller rinks, high schools, and recreation centers. Gentlemen of Desire and Black Tie Promotions organized these teen events and advertised by posting flyers. The *LA Times* called the parties "hit-and-run" because they operated without permits and adequate adult supervision. They moved on before police or parents could blame them for any resulting mayhem.

The Fancy Dancers Disco School started in Atlanta, Georgia, and later located in Columbus, bringing nightlife. The school gave lessons at the Citizens Action Club. Every urban center, large and small, has its own disco story.

3

Can't Stop the Music

The sensibility of an era is not only its most decisive, but its most perishable aspect.

From the 1966 "Notes on Camp" by Susan Sontag

New York-based music critic Vince Aletti, in 1973, used the term "disco" to describe a sound, rather than just a place. Aletti brought news of what was happening underground in the Loft and elsewhere. He saw in dancers, in the scene, the spontaneity in the music. DJ work was an option for musicians of the day. They were finding a throughline of different kinds of music to sustain a whole evening. The critics who were putting disco down early on were not dancing and had not experienced the tribal feeling that happened when the whole dance floor reacted as one. It was very exciting when there was not a formula involved, before "it became kitschified, narrowly defined, thump-thump-thump Euro disco" (Morley 2009).

Harold Rosenberg in his essay "Pop Culture: Kitsch Criticism" defined kitsch as something that persists after it is no longer considered in good taste. Susan Sontag took up Rosenberg's mantle in her famous "Notes on Camp." Disco has continued in the face of people's widespread loss of taste for it. We can call it kitsch. Kitsch deliberately designs to move us. For example, familiar disco or gay anthems elicit the predicted cheering and screaming in the expected atmosphere. The music in gay clubs, in the 1970s and beyond, validated shared sensibilities. It became socially useful and healed wounds for everyone, of any sexual orientation, who had experienced loss.

The labeling of disco as kitsch requires a trained eye and the sophistication of a camp perspective. Christopher Isherwood gives us the first published exploration of the word "camp" in his 1954 novel *The World in the Evening*. His character says he has heard people use the word in bars and in queer circles. Camping, a debased form of camp, is a "swishy boy ... with a feather boa, pretending to be Marlene Dietrich." By contrast, high camp has an underlying seriousness. Mozart is camp, Beethoven not. Ballet is camp about love. "You're expressing what is basically serious to you in terms of fun and artifice and elegance" (Isherwood 1952, 110).

Since these initial discussions of kitsch and camp, boundaries have blurred between high and low, good and bad, kitsch and art. We no longer consider them diametrically opposed. Artists have drawn on disco themes, while the dances and musical compilations have touched levels of artistry. Disco camp persists, while high and low borrow from each other.

Sontag said that homosexuals are the new aristocrats and bearers of special taste, at the vanguard of "camp." Sontag's essay helped introduce the 1970s pleasure principle and the notion that comfort and pleasure have a place in the arts and in our lives.

Milan Kundera explains kitsch as "the second tear." Club goers may experience a surge of emotion in response to the music and atmosphere of the club. Following this, they emote on how wonderful the feeling of enjoyment is "Over And Over," as in Sylvester's cover of the Ashford & Simpson song (lengthened in the 1979 12-inch disco version). Dancers want to stay at the club for many hours, even if that necessitates performance-enhancing drugs. They want to visit the club frequently and regularly.

In the 1970s, gay men led the procession after their long history of living in the closet. Americans were reeling from Vietnam. Men, especially, needed to be "where the happy people go" as the Trammps song instructs. A good many men had qualms about the Vietnam War—men who had enlisted, men who were drafted, and men who evaded the draft. Thousands of Americans and millions of Vietnamese died. Said Marty Angelo, creator of the TV show *Disco Step-by-Step*, "Coming out of the 60s, we thought we were gonna blow ourselves off the face of the earth. Back in those days, the Vietnam War, we barely made it

Disco essentials selected by Vince Aletti for the 1976 book *Dancing Madness:*

Barrabas: *Heart of the City* (Acto)

MFSB: *Love Is The Message, Universal Love* (Philadelphia International)

Bohannon: *Keep on Dancin', Insides Out* (Dakar)

B.T. Express: *Do It ('Till You're Satisfied), Non-Stop* (Scepter/Roadshow)

Ecstasy, Passion & Pain (Roulette)

First Choice: *Armed and Extremely Dangerous, The Player* (Philly Groove)

Gloria Gaynor: *Never Can Say Goodbye, Experience* (MGM)

Eddie Kendricks: *People . . . Hold On* (Tamia)

Love Unlimited: *Under the Influence Of . . .* (20th Century)

Van McCoy: *Disco Baby, The Disco Kid* (Avco)

George McCrae: *Rock Your Baby* (TK)

The Ritchie Family: *Brazil* (20th Century)

Silver Convention: *Save Me* (Midland International)

Donna Summer: *Love to Love You Baby* (Oasis)

Trammps (Golden Fleece)

through . . . and you're talkin' about getting on the dance floor?" (Angelo n.d.).

Discotheques provided opportunity for anaesthetization and entrance into a fantasy, netherworld. Think of the word (en)trance. But importantly, disco brought men onto the dance floor where they could find constructive help in the communion and physical expression of dancing.

Marshall McLuhan's *The Medium Is the Massage* had come out in 1967. The last word in his book title was a typographical error that he wanted to leave. Perhaps it foreshadowed the need for healing in the next decade. The medium "shapes and controls the scale and form of human association and action," he wrote (p. 9). In discos, dancers gave in to the power of the music on a tribal scale; they formed a kind of family and a microcosm of McLuhan's global village.

Aletti, in an article he wrote for *Rolling Stone* in August 1975, reported getting four or five invitations to new disco openings per day.

Two hundred or 300 new discos had been established in New York, and about 2,000 coast to coast. There he observed the new disco music evolving from 1960s dance records, Motown and Philly sound. Black rhythm and blues music took hold in the gay clubs at the margins of society. Said Aletti, "The spread of disco music, especially in the last year and a half ... outpaced even the growth of discos themselves." DJs favored a consistent danceable beat, longer songs, and breaks that allowed for shifts in mood. They were paying attention to the electronic mixing of the sound, which included traditional, orchestral instrumentation. Radio DJs were not as concerned with the technical mixing.

Catering to dancers on the floor, the club DJ chose longer songs with a hotter, brighter sound. David Mancuso would build a crescendo in the Loft, connecting records end to end, using two turntables. He found music no one had heard before and "broke" the records at his Loft parties. African polyrhythms were well suited to sweating it out on the dance floor and the masses' desire for individualism and release. Mancuso is best known for breaking "Soul Makossa" by Manu Dibango in 1973. Some consider it the first disco hit. He introduced the Spanish rock group Barrabas with "Wild Safari" and "Woman." He found a dance beat in other European imports and unexpected places like the rock music of Chicago, Doobie Brothers, and Led Zeppelin. Aletti called the Loft sound hard-driving, heavily percussive, frantic jungle music (Aletti 1975). Devoted Loft dancers were the mix of classes, colors, and sexual orientations that would become the disco ideal. The chemistry in the room determined the musical program, instead of the other way around. This improvisational approach would serve as the model for the Paradise Garage platform, among others.

The next year after "Soul Makossa" took New York by storm, Disco DJs, with their greater opportunities for experimentation, broke "Rock The Boat" by Hues Corporation, "Main Line" by Ashford & Simpson, "Dance Master" by Willie Henderson, and from Miami, George McCrea's "Rock Your Baby." The record labels also discovered that "disco patrons are affluent, trend-setting, and more than willing to spend their dollars on records." Continental Baths, Le Jardin, Better Days, and the Loft were "key spots to eye for a barometer of musical tastes" (Billboard 1974, 50).

Barry White's orchestral "Love's Theme" reached number one on the Billboard Hot 100 chart on February 9, 1974. White wrote it for the trio he managed—Sister Glodean, Linda Jones, and Diane Taylor, a.k.a. Love Unlimited—as an overture for the song "Under the Influence of Love." The contiguous pieces ran 8 minutes and 17 seconds, which gave the club DJ a few minutes to sit back and watch the sensation on the dance floor. The song set a trend for disco's longer cuts. The classic featured White's 40-piece Love Unlimited Orchestra (Bronson 2003, 357).

"Rock The Boat" was an afterthought on the Hues Corporation's first album *Freedom for the Stallion*. Fleming Williams is the lead singer who left the group just after, but was able to make "the mouthful of words in the . . . verses sing," said Hues founder Wally Holmes. Tom Sellers "came up with the little bit of reggae beat . . . and that drum beat was a very important part of making the record happen." RCA released it as a single after the positive response in clubs on the Las Vegas Strip, although radio DJs had not played it. After it became a hit on the dance floor, word spread, resulting in a sudden, mad rush to purchase the record. Fifty thousand copies were sold in advance of its radio debut on May 25, 1974. It hit number one on July 6 after six weeks of radio play (Bronson, 369).

Harry Wayne Casey and Richard Finch wrote and produced "Rock Your Baby" in less than an hour. Then next day they ran into George McCrae who completed the vocal tracks in two takes. McCrae's hit was next, entering the Billboard Hot 100 chart on June 1, 1974. Seven weeks later, it replaced "Rock The Boat" in the number one position (Bronson, 370).

Record companies then started recording single cuts on 12-inch discs played at 33 rpm to get the best reproduction at top volume. Giorgio Moroder's 17-minute remix of Donna Summer's "Love To Love You Baby," with its climactic moaning in the break, is the supreme example of extended ecstasy and Euro disco.

Long instrumental breaks were useful pauses for the DJ to weave in another song, matching the first rhythm. Then producers purposely built in breaks to accommodate the developing mixing techniques. After the Loft, Larry Levan and other DJs created intuitive programs in performances of slip-cueing or beat-on-beat mixing. They were swapping and blending records with similar beats per minute.

In a 1978 *Mixmaster* interview, editor Michael Gomes talked about the origins of disco. He recalled the Beatles' Magical Mystery Tour as an influence, with its overlay of sounds. He named Marvin Gaye's "What's Going On" as the first disco song because it reflected early disco's human concern. In the eponymous soul album, Gaye expressed his social consciousness. Cindy Lauper would cover the song in 1987, a few years after Gaye was shot and killed. But some disco music seemed to leave behind its roots in soul.

As early as April 1976, Aletti wrote in the *Village Voice* about a "shared hostility toward what has become known in the past year as 'disco.'" He cited an editorial "Death to Disco Shit" in the first issue of *Punk* magazine. Cheap "disco versions" were already on the market. Aletti deduced that the hostility came from "widespread unease and unfamiliarity" with the black popular music disco came out of. He also suggested that the critics, who put disco down, did not dance or go to clubs. He argued that the "won't quit" factor is part of the record's design and that the studio sophistication had not, in all cases, replaced feeling. He pointed out that the song "Dance Your Troubles Away" is not just for dancing, but also about dancing. It is about the healing power of dance. The title is a capsule of the lyric's imperative. Aletti deemed "Let's Groove" by Archie Bell, an anthem for the mid-1970s. It creates and invokes the sustained, expansive party spirit and captures the mood "of a time in which the dance floor has become a focus of social life and energy for so many of us." And "Maybe it isn't the music itself, but the demands of the music—the pressure of the beat and the lyrics: 'dance, dance, dance' 'get down, get down'—that arouses critical resistance" (Aletti 1976, 25–26).

Aletti had predicted that ready-made formulas would fall by the wayside because he saw so much creativity and experimentation in the clubs. But disco music did turn formulaic. Record pools were established where DJs could share the labels' new issues. In 1977, DJ Tom Lewis, based in rural Ballston Spa, New York, compiled a *Disco Bible* listing beats per minute. He advertised a computerized printout of over 1,500 songs and their bpm. He offered supplements with the latest fast-breaking hits. For $6.95, one could buy a list of 100 songs. The complete set was available for $49.95. An aspiring or experienced DJ no longer had to listen to and study each new song in order to plan a program. Bpm was no longer the property of a small group of pros. A core group of DJs, keepers of the craft of disco music, felt that the new facility came with a loss of quality. They feared that anyone, with or without musicality, could play DJ. The *Disco Bible* helped many more discos to open up, and people everywhere were dancing. At the same time, the craft of mixing music got ever more sophisticated and artful.

Bill Brewster, who wrote *Last Night a DJ Saved My Life*, called disco "the mothership of all of today's dance music," for example, house music and hip-hop. As hip-hop developed, creative DJs took their place as back-up bands. They continued the tradition: discovering, recycling, and remixing songs. The new turntablist cut and pasted, creating a bricolage of sounds.

Village People

The Village People's bubble-gum pop did not prevail in the gay clubs. But it did happen that homosexuals adopted songs like "YMCA" that were meant to express their culture. The 1980 Village People movie *Can't Stop the Music* is a cleaned-up portrait of the gay dance and music scene, palatable to all. It packaged and promoted the group of actor-singer-dancers. Ultimately, producers Jacques Morali and Henry Belolo wanted to sell music made for dance parties.

Morali and writer Belolo met in 1973. Belolo had just formed the record company Can't Stop Productions. They released a hit Ritchie Family record in 1975. A few years after that, they found Felipe Rose dancing at the West Village gay bar The Anvil, wearing a feather headdress. They created an "only in New York" snapshot, with Rose personifying New York's diverse Greenwich Village. Rose is the real hero, muse, and inspiration for the Village People.

Rose, however, was entirely serious. He had trained with the Ballet de Puerto Rico, having won a scholarship at 16. In the United States, he pursued a degree in business but got bored with the work and went back to studying dance. Meanwhile, he was making $80 a night performing at the bar in costumes. The "Indian" character was an expression of Rose's part–Native American heritage. He continued with the Village People into the twenty-first century.

The producers saw an Anvil patron dressed as a cowboy, watching Rose dance. They imagined the Village People, a group of singers dressed as masculine stereotypes and appealing to gay and straight men and women. They hired a group of models to pose with Rose for the cover of the 1977 debut album *Village People*. The centerpiece, a parked motorcycle, completed the brand and concept. Actual musicians would follow. Lead singer Victor Willis, who had worked on Ritchie Family songs, dressed as a policeman. Session singers filled in the gaps.

Belolo's songs for the debut were about U.S. locales with strong gay communities—Hollywood, San Francisco, Greenwich Village, Fire Island. "San Francisco" was a hit. DJs played the 12-inch discs and dancers responded. When the album was a success, they held an audition to create a performing group. By putting ads in local papers, they found good-looking gay men with mustaches who could sing and dance. The group's composition would change over the course of three peak albums and for the life of the group. The original six included Glen Hughes, a toll collector on the Brooklyn Battery Tunnel who had never sang or danced. He did have a spectacular mustache and he could satirize the leather man/biker. His costume brought gay fetish attire out in the open.

David Hodo had played a chorus boy on stage. The 150-pound actor was hired in 1977 and suspended disbelief as the Construction Worker. "When I'm onstage I live the fantasy," he said in a *Can't Stop the Music* DVD bonus interview.

Randy Jones had graduated from the North Carolina School of the Arts and danced with Agnes DeMille's company. After moving to New York, he modeled for the gay cultural magazine *After Dark*, toured with Grace Jones, and danced in her club act. He answered the Can't Stop ad and won the cowboy role on the 1978 *Macho Man* album. The next recording was *Cruisin'*, with "YMCA" on it, and Alex Briley dressed as a soldier on the cover. Briley had been a choirboy, a professional jazz singer, and had appeared with Willis in an off-Broadway show. The next year, they released *Go West* with the hit "In the Navy". After that, Ray Simpson replaced Willis as the military man. He appears as the military man, in the movie *Can't Stop the Music* and on the 1979 double album *Live and Sleazy*.

Allan Carr of *Grease* fame produced the movie *Can't Stop the Music*. It was filmed in San Francisco and Greenwich Village. The Director Nancy Walker never made another feature film, but she did direct a few episodes of *Mary Tyler Moore* (IMBD n.d.). She is famous for playing Rhoda's Mother Ida Morgenstern on that show and on *Rhoda*. She died of lung cancer at age 69 in 1992. Hughes died of lung cancer in 2001, and Morali of AIDS complications in 1991. The group continued to tour after the movie and produced occasional singles.

Glen Hughes resented the duplicitous outcome of *Can't Stop the Music*. On the one hand, the songs were meant to please gay fans, yet the characters' homosexuality was played down to appeal to the

The Village People. (Photofest)

masses. "Our popularity is being used as a commodity. They are not recreating the Village People experience" (Mangels 2002). It was a thinly veiled circle of exploitation.

Newsweek called the movie "the first all singing, all dancing horror film." And *Film Review* called it "the box office calamity of the summer." The soundtrack reached only number 47 on the charts. When it came out in July 1980, the disco era was gone. The title had been *Discoland*, but that was changed as people suddenly turned against disco. The new title exemplified the new, necessary attitude among dancers and club goers that disco was, in fact, unstoppable, whatever you want to call it.

About the third album *Cruisin'*, Robert Christgau said, "I've never been capable of resisting music this silly." By their 1981 album *Renaissance*, they were trying new wave, but few could accept the change.

Glam and Disco

In Randy Jones's book *Macho Man*, he and cowriter Mark Bego argue that the glam rock movement was important in bringing about the 1970s loosening of taboos around sexual behavior. David Bowie was openly gay or bisexual and appropriated gay ball attire for his shows. He performed in makeup, glitter, feather boas, and dresses. Both he and his wife, Angela, were trained dancers. When they went out, David danced like a jazz dancer, said Angela in her memoir *Free Spirit*. When a reporter from *Melody Maker* magazine asked him if he was gay, he replied in the affirmative. This placed him in the maelstrom of gay liberation and encouraged him to make a statement of his homo-sexuality. Young people around the world sent him letters thanking him. On and off stage he offered a revolutionary message of gay pride. Angela and David Bowie had an open marriage and it did not last, but they were a team. Angela made the costumes. They had a child, Zowie. Bowie, presenting as a bisexual, androgynous space alien, was a pioneer in the field of rock-theater. The movie *2001: A Space Odyssey* inspired him. When Bowie's *Young Americans* came out, musi-cian and rock writer Lester Bangs criticized it for "going disco" and for "going black" (Echols 2010, 177). Bowie is peripheral, but significantly influenced the emergence of disco. Nile Rodgers, leader of the classic disco group Chic, produced Bowie's album *Modern Love* in 1983.

Lou Reed was also important to the disco ethos. His 1972 "Walk on the Wild Side" from his album *Transformer* (Bowie is a producer) is about transvestites, hustlers, and other characters from Andy Warhol's Factory. He was in Warhol's group, The Velvet Underground, until 1970. When Reed explained his homosexuality to his parents, they had him see a doctor who subjected him to electroshock therapy. Thirteen years later, in 1983, he wrote a song about it, "Kill Your Sons."

While disco was a male-centered phenomenon, girl groups were forming with feminism. A case in point is the Runaways, a group of California Valley girls who got together under Kim Fowley's manage-ment. This glam rock group was the brainchild of Joan Jett and producer-director Fowley.

Fowley's concept recalls the way Belolo and Morali manufactured the Village People. Fowley and Jett plucked 15-year-old blonde bomb-shell Cherie Currie from a nightclub because of her cool style. They saw potential "rock 'n roll authority" in her. "All you have to do is sing and look pretty," Jett said, and Currie writes in *Neon Angel* (Currie 2010). Currie could sing. She had also danced on *American Bandstand*. The group was a meeting of the minds. Fowley was the father figure, and critic Robert Christgau, among others, called it exploitative.

Their debut *The Runaways* came out in 1976 with the hit "Cherry Bomb." *Queens of Noise* followed in 1977. Some say their music rebelled against the orchestral proto-disco music that was becoming popular in the early 1970s. However, as Jett said to Katie Rich at the Sundance Festival, "it was more about rebelling against what people tell you you can [or can't] do" (Jett 2010). They were teens, and they were breaking the social and sexual taboos that say girls cannot make rock and roll music. Reviewing their debut album, Kris Needs said, "The only all-girl punk-rock band" was promising, after admitting he had ogled the seductive cover photo (Needs 1976). The graphic teaser across the cover of *Crawdaddy,* October 1976, read, "Teen Lust, Power Chords, Quay Lewdness."

In the United States and Japan, teen girls came to see them, and Currie sent a message about the sexual power they could harness with their adolescent hormones. *Spin* magazine called *Runaways: Live in Japan* the sound of the 1970s.

As two historians put it, "Somebody was finally saying what it was like to be a teenager in the 1970s. And to make it even better, these were girls saying it." The teen clubs they had played in succumbed to commercialization by 1977, and prevailing patriarchal beliefs subsumed their ideals. In other words, disco took over. The male-dominated 1970s rock press wrote off *Cherry Bomb* as a "slutty, manu-factured, novelty act" (J. Rosenberg and Garafolo 1988).

Currie prided herself as the first rocker to dance on stage in a corset, a trend that Madonna is credited with setting much later. The Run-aways performed ideas of liberation. However, they were paid with a child's allowance, lived on hamburgers, Coca-Cola, cocaine, diet pills, pain pills, and Quaaludes. They worked like dogs and were *called* dogs by their surrogate father, Fowler, who created them as a band.

Disco stars Grace Jones, Madonna, and Michael Jackson came to disco with grounding in glam rock sensibility.

The Bee Gees Heat up the Celluloid Dance Floor

The Bee Gees core, twins Robin and Maurice, and the eldest Barry, had been earning a reputation for skimming contemporary rhythm and blues songs. Crossover was the norm, though, and even the point of disco. Philly soul, James Brown, and Roy Ayers exchanged sounds. Bowie was dancing at discos like the Loft with Mick Jagger and other

musicians. Philly soul influenced Bowie's 1975 *Young Americans*, especially its proto-disco song "Fame." It still lacked the four-on-the-floor
beat that disco requires. Sylvester hung with Bowie when he was in
Europe from 1973 to 1975. Bowie, Sylvester, and the Bee Gees featured
falsetto vocals. Brown, Bowie, the Bee Gees, and Sylvester covered
and appropriated each other's sounds. The Stones even worked on a
cover of "Shame, Shame, Shame," but they never recorded it. The
1975 Shirley & Company song puts listeners to shame if they can't
dance "too."

The Bee Gees are the Brothers Gibb. Musicologist Alice Echols
called their music "blue-eyed disco soul." The group was in a rut
and had all but disbanded. They were plagued with legal problems
and awash in drugs and alcohol when Robert Stigwood brought them
on board for *Saturday Night Fever*.

Although the brothers were not well respected by their colleagues at
that point in time, *Main Course* and "Jive Talkin" did impress them.
Barry commented in *Disco Madness*, "People wanted to dance. They're
not listening to the lyrics anymore. After we recorded it, everyone
said it was disco. We didn't even know what disco was at that time"
(Peck 1976). Since Atlantic Records wanted to maximize appeal and
sales, the cover had no photo of the brothers. Since the music could
be mistaken for that of a black group, the company wanted to capital-
ize on that ambiguity. Thus, said Echols, "Disco was altering the
dynamics of cross-over."

The Bee Gees created the 1976 *Children of the World*, including the
classic disco anthem "You Should Be Dancing," with engineer Karl
Richardson and arranger, keyboardist Albhy Galuten. It featured
piercing falsetto and 18 pounding percussion tracks. Now working
under Stigwood's label RSO, the group hid away in the Chateau near
Paris where Bowie's *Ziggy Stardust* and classic rock albums of early
1970s had been recorded. The Gibb brothers have given varying
accounts of how long it took them to create five *Saturday Night Fever*
songs, ranging from a few hours to five weeks. The soundtrack sold
more than 30 million copies and most agree that the music deserves
about half the credit for the movie's success.

With Richardson and Galuten, they refined the sound with overdubs.
Galuten may have invented the disco drum loop when they recycled a
bar from one of the songs, "Night Fever." Barry Gibb and Galuten
applied it to "Stayin' Alive" and "More than a Woman" when their

drummer left early for a family emergency. They liked that particular bar and the loop because it sounded insistent but not mechanical.

"Night Fever" came about when Barry Gibb heard keyboardist Blue Weaver playing with a disco version of a Percy Faith song "Theme from *A Summer Place.*" A British critic later found that tune in Barry White's "Love's Theme." The world is our oyster, say the Bee Gees in "Night Fever," and the feeling is meant to be contagious. The slow ballad "How Deep Is Your Love" completed their contribution to the movie.

Bee Gees songs in *Saturday Night Fever*:

"If I Can't Have You" (performed by Yvonne Elliman)

"How Deep Is Your Love"

"Night Fever"

"Stayin' Alive"

"More Than A Woman" (performed by Tavares)

"You Should Be Dancin' "

Other songs in the movie: "Salsation" and "Night on Disco Mountain" by David Shire, "K-Jee" by MFSB, "Fifth of Beethoven" by Walter Murphy, "Disco Inferno" by Trammps, "Open Sesame" by Kool and the Gang, "Disco Duck" and "Dr. Disco" by Rick Dees, and "Boogie Shoes" by KC and the Sunshine Band.

Disco-Tex, also known as Monti Rock III, and Bronx-born Joseph Montanez Jr. played the Odyssey DJ in *Fever*. He had been dancing in discos for 12 years when *Rolling Stone* interviewed him for *Dancing Madness*. He broke his 1974 hit "Get Dancin'" by performing it in discos.

The brothers mentored their fourth, much younger sibling, Andy Gibb, who would become a teen idol with his own 1978 album *Shadow Dancing*. The title, platinum track was number one for seven weeks. He suffered from depression, cocaine addiction, and heart problems, which caused his death at age 30.

Disco was falling out of favor, to put it mildly. Attention was focused on Andy in the 1980s. The Bee Gees sued producer Stigwood for mismanagement in 1980. Three years later, they composed the soundtrack for *Fever* sequel movie *Stayin' Alive*, which was a flop. The album went platinum, but it was not as popular as *Saturday Night Fever*.

The Bee Gees won seven Grammy awards including Lifetime and Legend awards, and Best Album of the Year for *Saturday Night Fever* in 1978. In 1997, they were inducted into the Rock and Roll Hall of Fame. Maurice died in 2003. *Rolling Stone* magazine described the Bee Gees, pop-disco sound as celestial glamour recalling Glen Miller and Frank Sinatra (Holden 1978).

"It took the Bee Gees to really bring disco to the forefront of the music industry with their *Saturday Night Fever* LP" (*The Modesto Bee* 1979). But Barry Gibb did not identify with disco then. He told the *Bee* reporter that to follow, the group wanted to produce Barbara Streisand's next album, "if they can pull her away from disco."

Discofication

The German studio group Silver Convention, founded by Silvester "Silver" Levay and Michael Kunze, released *Save Me* in 1975, ushering in Euro disco. Brian Chin, in his *Disco Box* notes, called the title song's scant lyrics "words that scamper around the music like a flirt's scent."

"Fly, Robin, Fly," also on *Save Me*, was the number one hit single for three weeks that year. The five-minute song has only six words (including the two in the title). Said Kunze, "I realized all you needed was a strong bassline, a snappy snare sound, and some coloring. You want to think, 'What will make people dance?' " (Peck 1976). They followed up with "Get Up And Boogie" in 1976. The Silver Convention Vocalists then went solo with their Americanized names Linda Thompson ("Lady Bump") and Penny McClean ("Oh, What A Night").

Musicians climbed on the bandwagon. James Brown is perhaps the most notorious. He came out with the 1975 album *Everybody's Doin' the Hustle* and the single "Hustle!!! (Dead On It)." The lyrics express Brown's observation of the dance craze. It was a spectacular synergy of sound and bodily performance from an artist at his peak. But Brown ran into big trouble over the song. Tala Andre-Marie, the blind, Congolese guitarist from The Black Tigers, successfully sued him for plagiarizing his tune "Hot Koki." Yet, Congolese Afro-pop artists were listening to Brown in the early 1970s, and Andre-Marie cites him as an influence (Winders 2006).

The "Hustle!!! (Dead On It)" lyrics describe Brown's concatenation of sexualized movements, some from Hustle dance and some from other disco dances like the Bump, with creative liberties added. His imperative, do the *nasty* Hustle, was misunderstood. He meant sexy, real, not pretty. There is so much power and musicality in this master's dance. His is very different from that of the young Latin club dancers who watched their parents do the Cha-Cha or Mambo and updated the steps and the poses for the popular songs of the 1970s. Brown apparently wanted to own any and all the new dance crazes.

Brown had his own particular beat that was very heavy on the "one." He teaches it to us in his song "Dead On It." He did not offer lightness and happiness. He did insist on the blackness in disco. He asks himself, in the song, in all honesty, if he will be able to get up after he gets down.

As his sales were slipping in the disco era, he tried again to get into the market with his 1979 album *The Original Disco Man*, reminding us of disco's roots in soul and funk, but it only reached number 152 on the charts. Nevertheless, people dancing the commemorative James Brown mass line Hustle today, with fast feet sliding in each direction, immortalize him. Songs like "Give It Up" became disco dance floor classics. YouTube videos of his live performances of it leave little doubt why. His dancing is an extension of his funk and soul, one-of-a-kind music, and he entrances us with it. He belongs to the cannon of disco-era divas who speak to some aspect of the collective human spirit.

JB wanted to take on disco, and he was a political artist singing about civil rights, peace, and love. He wrote the 1968 song "Say It Loud (I'm Black And I'm Proud)" in response to Martin Luther King's death. It is an important song with no thread of militancy, but evidently, the simple fact that we're all human beings was too radical for some. The song is a release from oppression. "My freedom [was] meant to represent all black people's freedom" (Brown 2005, 221).

He considers "Sex Machine" his first disco song. He performed it before its release in 1975. Brown had gone through considerable pain when his son Teddy, who could sing and dance and had a group Teddy & The Torches, died in a car accident. He drowned the pain in the intense pleasure of music and dance. Brown had just signed with Polydor Records when the label crossed into disco.

Later, problems with drugs, drink, and the IRS got the better of him. Would-be fans reviled him for supporting Richard Nixon. Charges of wife battering and sexual harassment turned the rest away. Women's rights advocates protested when Brown was up for his Kennedy Center honor, awarded to him in December 2003. The love he sought was an even more distant object. His wife Adrienne died on the operating table while undergoing plastic surgery in 1996. Brown's autobiography is something of a pleading for understanding, like the song he wrote half a century earlier, "Please Please Please." His lover has done him wrong, but he is asking her not to go as he loves her so. Likewise, the autobiography is not an apology. In his autumn, he turned to God and wrote that he felt closest to Moses. "I still feel the need to help my people find a better place in the world and I do it by looking up and asking for advice from the almighty" (Brown 2005).

Brown died on Christmas Day 2006, at age 73. Although he had more than his share of troubles and was cast as a pariah in his day, he paved the way for black entertainers and black pride. He was super bad, in a bad way. He often saw others copying his moves, even Elvis. Many did. There is an element of truth in his self-proclaimed title *The Original Disco Man*. Unlike the Bee Gees, Brown did not feel too cool for disco.

It was songwriter Van McCoy and the orchestra he formed, the Soul City Symphony, who released the Grammy award-winning single "The Hustle," the last-minute addition to his nearly completed disco album *Disco Baby*. This song is full of the decorum on the dance floor that came with the new dance called the Hustle. This natural companion for the line dance, the vanilla L.A. Hustle, is very lyrical after its initial, repeated imperative to "do it." To a room full of couples dancing one form of the Hustle or another, the song expresses the manners associated with ballroom dancing. McCoy understood that aspect of the Latin or New York Hustle dance, if not its intricate steps and its cool passion.

The common story is that McCoy sent his partner Charles Kipp to see the new dance at the Adam's Apple club. DJ David Todd had been urging him to come over. Kipp came back to the studio with some dancers, and McCoy was inspired. It reminded him of ballroom dancing, and he "loved graceful dancing," he told *Essence Magazine* (Bronson 2003, 410). Then, with just an hour of studio time left, he "threw together" the song. It was number one on the pop charts on July 26, 1975, and it is credited with nothing less than bringing touch dancing back to the fore. Additionally, the song piqued Nik Cohn's journalist curiosity about a possible social dance trend that no one had covered (Echols 2010, 161).

The development of disco Hustle in its popular form, as seen on celluloid, came from these second-hand sources, so it's no wonder it didn't exactly match the Hustle dance developed by dancers in the small clubs around New York City and spread by professionals and semi-professionals in the burgeoning discos.

Two years later, when the movie came out and disco had exploded, McCoy said he no longer wanted to be "marketed as a specific product." He would never match the success of "The Hustle" even though he came out with a stylish sequel called "Keep On Hustlin'." He died on July 6, 1979, of a heart attack in Englewood Hospital in the New Jersey town where John Travolta grew up. "The Hustle" song and dance lives on at dance clubs and on YouTube.

Cuban Flautist and band leader Jose Fajardo recorded "C'mon Baby Do the Latin Hustle" in 1975 on the Coco label. It has soft disco drums, electric guitar bassline, synthesizer, female backup vocal harmonies; repetitive, simple, entrancing melody, pop strings, and brass; it is uptempo, imperative, and has almost no lyrics beyond the title. This Hustle song is meant to accompany dancers doing the authentic Latin Hustle couples dance born in the 1970s. Fajardo played in Island, Miami, and New York clubs, at first in a Charenga style and then popularizing Pachengo, with its more assertive rhythms. He played at El Palladium in the mid-1950s and again after 1969 (Pareles 2001).

The list of artists making music for the Hustle dance does not end here. In 1975, Salsoul Orchestra released "Salsoul Hustle," an upbeat, completely instrumental, 8-minutes-plus, with the same ruffled, synthesized, melodic passages that inspire quick turns. It is heavy on the "one" for the step back that launches each repeating sequence of the dance. Salseros call steps with weight shifts "Breaks."

Tavares, five brothers from Boston, wanted to "Give the people what they want" in their disco hit "It Only Takes A Minute," an uptempo song on their 1975 album *In the City*. Meanwhile, the Trammps came from Philly Soul to "discover " disco.

Philly Sound

In August 1968, songwriters and fledgling producers Kenny Gamble and Leon Huff were testing the sound at a brand new studio on 212 North Twelfth Street in Philadelphia. They brought in musician friends, including Ronnie Baker, Norman Harris, and Earl Young, and recorded "We Don't Need No Music" by the Landslides and Ruth McFadden's "Get A Woman" and "Rover, Rover." They are some of the first hits called Philly sound. And the music-makers stayed together because, as producer Wheeldon McDougal said, "They was all the same kind of guys. We was considered squares" (Dmitri 2010).

Producer Theodore "T" Life discovered sixteen-year-old Evelyn "Champagne" King singing in the bathroom of Sigma Studios. She was working there with her mother after-hours as a part-time cleaner. (Photofest)

Five years later, these musicians, performing in Harold Melvyn & The Blue Notes, recorded a groundbreaking version of the 6/8 Gamble & Huff ballad "The Love I Lost." Percussionist Young recalled how he "kicked it to the floor four times." Boom—boom—boom—boom on the big bass drum, pushing the pedal to the floor, would come to be known as four-on-the-floor. Young used a 2/4 tempo on the snare drum and an eighth note on the sock cymbal. That percussion solution and Baker's synched guitar bassline are signatures of disco. Their uptempo version of "The Love I Lost" (in the 1973 album *Black and Blue*) and "Bad Luck" in *To Be True* (1975) are two quintessential disco songs that emerged from Philly sound. Robert Christgau praised The Blue Notes's lead singer Teddy Pendergrass's "tender strength" and singled out "Bad Luck" as a song about blacks' suffering and poverty. Young later founded the Trammps with Harris and Baker. Trammps cut two albums in 1976— *Where the Happy People Go*, with the disco favorite title track, and then *Disco Inferno* with its extended dance tracks including a 10-minute and 54-second version of the title song—from Sigma Sound Studios.

MFSB (Mother, Father, Sister, Brother), the O'Jays, Lou Rawls, Archie Bell and The Drells, Patti LaBelle, and Phyllis Hyman also recorded on the Philadelphia International label that Gamble and Huff started in 1971.

In 1973, MFSB's T.S.O.P (The Sound of Philadelphia)—with its elements of R&B, Soul, gospel, funk, orchestral, and big-band sounds—became the *Soul Train* theme song. That year, billboard used the term "disco hit." That year, "Soul Makossa" crossed over from the clubs to the Top 40 charts.

The next year, the Hues Corporation's "Rock The Boat" was a hit. Archie Bell and The Drells' 1975 hit was "Dance Your Troubles Away" on the eponymous LP. By that pivotal year, record companies had established dedicated disco labels. Polydor crossed over. The West Coast had Casablanca. T.K. Disco made special 12-inch records for DJs and discotheques.

Club patrons heard the songs first. DJs broke songs in the disco era. That is, they were not selling until club goers ran to the stores to pick up the records they heard and danced to the night before. The trend would be toward longer, single songs on 12-inch discs made especially for the clubs, with breaks to create crescendos of suspense on the dance floor and to create a place for mixing in another cut. The DJ juxtaposed records to shift the mood or create dramatic narrative for the evening. The idea was for listeners, club goers, to have a good time—and that meant dancing. Listening to the dance songs without dancing did not work at all. Christgau said he got bored during the breaks.

Disco Divas, Gay Anthems

Gay clubs brought in the disco era along with nurturing female divas. Bette Midler's emotional songs poured out in the Continental Baths to an accepting and generous audience of men. Robert Christgau said he had "been entranced by her show many times." He gave a high rating to the 1972 *The Divine Miss M*. As the first den mother at the baths, she played to a captive audience of men in towels, backed up by Barry Manilow on piano. She sang old Andrews Sisters' songs and rock 'n' roll camp classics. In 1972, "Friends" by Buzzy Linheart and Mark "Moogy" Klingman became her theme song at the baths (Bego 2009, 176). Christgau later criticized her for modulating her wackiness in later albums and called her "just another pop singer." But in her 1977 *Live at Last*, he liked the "overripe" singing in her tearjerker "Hello In There" and its preface of "campy, unkind patter."

Gay anthems cited by Mark Bego and Randy Jones in their 2009 book *Macho Man* include the 1972 David Bowie recording of Mott the Hoople's song "All The Young Dudes" and from Bowie's '74 *Diamond Dogs* album, "Rebel, Rebel." Bette Midler's "My Knight In Black Leather" in 1979 is "the ultimate leatherman song." At the club New York, New York, after the Supremes's Mary Wilson went solo in 1977, she introduced "Red Hot" by Frank Busey and John Duarte. "[It] was the way that every gay boy on the disco dance floor felt about themselves" (Bego 2009). In 1979, Nile Rodgers and Bernard Edwards from Chic teamed up with Sister Sledge to record the song that would be the ultimate gay anthem, across the board. "We Are Family" made everyone on the dance floor feel like a star, even if it did not have that danceable disco beat. The song spoke to the many homosexuals whose families of origin had disowned them. They found new, chosen families on the dance floor.

Patti Labelle and Nona Hendrix (songwriter) with "You Turn Me On," Thelma Houston, Loleatta Holloway, Candi Staton, and Gloria Gaynor are favorite disco divas from back in the day. Donna Summer's 1975 "Love To Love You, Baby" was a groundbreaking expression of female pleasure and fantasy. A stomping bass drum beat was the male response to Summer's four-minute vocal orgasm. The dancer strove to complete the picture. Gaynor's "I Will Survive" is the most famous late gay anthem. According to Tim Lawrence, Gaynor had to learn to dance because there was a lot of downtime in the instrumental breaks of her songs. Diana Ross recorded a later version of "I Will Survive" and her own disco hit "I'm Comin' Out." These Divas performed live, and their recordings continue to enchant men in gay dance halls.

Gaynor's 1974 "Honeybee" was her disco start. Then people found it hard to keep from dancing and singing along to Tom Moulton's mix of "Never Can Say Goodbye." It has the built-in instrumental break, so does "Reach Out (I'll Be There)" and the danceable ballad "Jive Time (Casanova Brown)" with its chanted fable of meeting the bad boy on the dance floor, its memorable squeal of delight, and a sax solo. "I Will Survive" left no doubt in 1978 that Gaynor was "Queen of Disco." Gaynor called the song an antidepressant. It was not only a gay anthem, it was also a women's anthem, advocating self-reliance. It was a message to straight, abusive men that women could survive without them. Gaynor now offers an "I Will Survive"

Donna Summer performing at Universal Amphitheater in Los Angeles, August 11, 1979. (Associated Press)

30-year anniversary CD. In 1980, the only year with a category Best Disco Recording, Gaynor and producers Dino Fekaris and Freddie Perren won a Grammy for "I Will Survive." Over seven million viewers have watched a three-minute, 1979 Polygram song promotion featuring Gaynor and the Harlem skater Sheila Reid of the Village Wizards on YouTube.

Grace Jones inspired each dancer to crop his hair short and become a "Slave To The Rhythm." She embodied, with her tall, thin, clean, and vertical stature, the imperative for gay men to allow pleasure and penetration, to succumb to control and enslavement. In Jones's music, the beat embodies desire. She was the ultimate model for pleasure-seeking club goers, gay and straight, who were reinventing themselves in costume and dancing roles. She glorified artificiality and androgyny. Jones straddled rock and disco, but her songs' romantic instrumentations and arrangements made them disco anthems.

Jones, Gaynor, and especially Donna Summer's songs suggest autoerotic ecstasy. The female orgasm with its repeating peaks found expression through these divas and in disco music. Gaynor in particular weathered the storm of AIDS at the end of the disco era with her anthem "I Will Survive." Walter Hughes wrote, "For a few years in the late '80s, it seemed as if disco would die of its own disease" (Hughes 1993). Instead, the dancing continued, and it became a strategy for survival.

Disc Jockeys' Disco

In gay dance clubs, DJs used a palette of classic disco songs—R&B, funk, Philly sound and soul, sounds rooted in African-American experience—and layers of electronic manipulations to create all-night programs.

New York DJ Terry Noel played records back-to-back on two turntables at Arthur's in 1965. A few years later, he was at Salvation II. Francis Grasso took over when Noel showed up late for work, tripping. Grasso was playing Motown, Creedence Clearwater, and "96 Tears" for straight couples. He moved to Seymour and Shelly's Sanctuary and played for straight couples until after Stonewall, when new owners took over and kept the women out to create a gay sanctuary. Grasso is the DJ in the movie *Klute* and worked at that club for about a year. He invented the technique known as slip-cueing (stopping the record with his thumb). Thus, DJs consider him the father of modern disc jockeying. He garnered a following by engineering a narrative experience through his smoothly segueing musical program of R&B and rock—James Brown's "Hot Pants" or "Sex Machine" and "Whole Lotta Love" by Led Zeppelin. He credits his success to musicality and the fact that he started out as a dancer. He was a go-go boy, dancing on a platform to a live band in Greenwich Village, New York (Grasso 1999).

Tom Moulton, the legendary mixer, walked onto the Sandpiper floor to see how dancers were responding to his tapes in 1975. "Free Man" is Moulton's famous remixed gay anthem. Historian Tim Lawrence credits Moulton with introducing dance music to symphonic structures. In the early 1970s, DJ Bobby Guttadero reigned at Le Jardin. Meanwhile, Tom Savarese started at 12 West in March 1975, and the club was a favorite haunt for DJs on nights off.

With increasingly sophisticated equipment, the DJ was mixing songs live. David Mancuso had a simple mixing technique and a good sound system. He created scores that set the mood for the racially mixed crowd of hard-core dancers at his exclusive, private, legendary Loft parties. Eastern philosophies of Enlightenment, the stages of a chemical high, and a quest for pure sound guided his program, as well as gems he found in friends' gifts of albums or odd records he bought. Mancuso suggested a record pool for DJs to exchange information and set professional standards. Sixty-five founding members signed up. The Loft was important as the notable DJ-owned dancing establishment and as the place that inspired another DJ, Larry Levan. Michael Brody built the well-known Paradise Garage around Levan. His legend looms large, as he prefigured the future of dance music in a distinct genre called "garage." Today his music is on iTunes.

While Nicky Siano was DJ at the Gallery, Larry Levan was decorator and promoter. At Continental Baths in the Ansonia Hotel, in 1973, he got his chance. There he worked with Frankie Knuckles who followed Levan and went on to pioneer house music. In the mid-1970s in Richard Long's Soho Place, a showcase for his mixing equipment, Brody heard Levan and envisioned him in the booth at his new club. The Garage opened in 1977. There, Levan was an *artiste* with a soul and R&B-based individual style. He mixed with crossover so that the records "talked to each other" (Cheren 2000). This is the cross-phasing that was used to achieve the dreamy vision state in *Saturday Night Fever* during the song "More Than a Woman." He communed with his flock on the floor, paying attention to the song's lyrics. Meanwhile, he was upgrading his turntable needles and inserting other tricks to achieve his hallmark clarity. Many consider Levan the all-time greatest DJ, although some fault him for sloppy mixes and over-loudness. He took risks. For example, he played a single song that he felt was particularly apt, for one hour. He restructured songs and inserted music from other genres. Despite his unpredictability, people took what they liked about his style—dark, soulful, bottom-heavy, jazzy, and his way of building the tension and stretching the beat with his unique dubbing technique—and branded it "garage," originally, a New York City sound.

Like the Loft, the Garage was a serious social dancers club, but much larger. Levan presided over a first, themed Night of the Bats party, where he broke a bright, clear remix of Evelyn "Champagne" King's "Shame." Word spread immediately to gay discos in other cities. Then, industry people saw sales of the record swell. As a result, they paid more attention to the musical tastes of first responders in gay underground discos (Cheren 2000, 209). Later came the Fire Down Below party and the extravagantly emulated Tut Tut Tut. It featured statues of Ramses and parchment invites. Karen Young gave an electric debut of her new hit "Hot Shot" *a cappella* when Levan couldn't find the instrumental track for it. The underground Garage on King Street closed in 1987, and Levan died five years later from congenital heart failure, exacerbated by drug use (Apple n.d.). By then, "Drugs were over the top at every club and at every label," said Mel Cheren, founder of West End Records and one-time mate of Michael Brody.

The smattering (at best) of women in gay clubs consisted of industry professionals and/or great dancers, and only a few worked in the inner sanctum of the DJ's booth. Judy Weinstein had started an alternative (to David Mancuso's) record pool called For the Record. She was welcome in Levan's booth.

DJ Bert Lockett went by the moniker "Dyke on the Mike." She started at the uptown Manhattan bar Ernie's. She played at the lesbian bar Bonnie and Clyde's, where she thought, wrongly, that she would find respect. She is best known as the inaugural DJ at Better Days, when it opened in 1972 as a gay bar and dance club. But when the owner's wife asked for a request, Lockett refused. Tee Scott, a garage-style pioneer, took over and brought in Frankie Knuckles, who would create the Chicago house music style. Scott produced the garage classics "Tee's Happy," "Jazzy Rhythms," and Russ Brown's "Gotta Find A Way." He died of colon cancer in 1995 at age 47.

By the end of the 1970s, dance halls were ready for Sharon White. She is the first woman resident DJ at the Saint. She is one of the few women who went to the Saint. The lack of women present in the DJ and club scene did not put her off. White has said she was always treated with respect and paid the same wages as her male counterparts. "I tried to make people aware of the fact that GENDER has nothing to do with your ability to present music," she said to Discoguy in an undated interview on the Web site disco-disco.com. White worked at the popular lesbian bar Sahara. She was also a guest DJ at Paradise Garage and the *only* female DJ ever to have worked there. She is unusual in considering both clubs among her favorites. In the twenty-first century, she worked at Pavilion in Fire Island Pines and at New York parties.

Sharon White Anthems via disco-disco.com

Saint anthems:

"Total Control" and "Hold On To My Love" (Jimmy Ruffin)

"Sweet Dreams" and "Love Is A Stranger" (Eurythmics)

Garage anthems:

"Love Is The Message" (MFSB)

"Weekend" (both the Phreek and the Class Action versions)

"Peanut Butter/Lock It Up" (Gwen Guthrie)

"Slave To The Rhythm" (Grace Jones)

A more hi-tech, new-agey sound prevailed at Flamingo, Tenth Floor, circuit parties, the Saint, and its ilk (see Saint or Garage, pp. 13–17). More sophisticated and expensive technology, along with grander spaces and spectacles, enabled a gradual evolution toward the Euro disco, sleaze, hi-NRG, and then to the house sounds that comprise early twenty-first-century dance music. The music writer Brian Chin took over Vince Aletti's Disco File column in *Record World*. Chin also

Classic disco did not become extinct with the increase in electronic sounds. The various musical threads in disco's evolution continue to serve a purpose. For example, the funkier African-American Philly sound in the Pointer Sisters' first 1973 hit "Yes We Can-Can," by Allen Toussaint, was recalled in 2008 when President Obama adopted the three words as a slogan. His mantra referred to and renewed the song's message of brotherhood, hope for the future, and our part in it.

Obama's New Hampshire campaign speech inspired a new, hopeful "Yes We Can" by Will.i.am of the Black-eyed Peas. The song served as a new, grassroots anthem for the age of Obama. It reprised the call for optimism and effort on the part of African-Americans and the black pride of the 1970s. To date, the 2008 "Yes We Can" YouTube music video was viewed 20 million times.

wrote liner notes for the exemplary Rhino *Disco Box* collection and others. He called the 1978 hit "Come To Me," by Montreal native France Joli, the turning point from traditional Fire Island disco, or classic disco, to the more progressive dance music of the 1980s.

Electronic hi-NRG is prevalent in large, gay, urban dance extravaganzas like the ones DJ Billy Carroll ministers to. Back in the day, "Never Can Say Goodbye" and Donna Summer's "I Feel Love" are Saint anthems Carroll heard as a guest at a White Party. He remembers "a moment" where the music segued into an introduction for Melba Moore who appeared magically from behind a panel and sang "Pick Me Up, I'll Dance" to 4,000 or 5,000 screaming men in elegant white. "She looked like a princess in a white, glittery, flowing gown. She was a big dance star at the time and there she was, singing for all her gay fans." Saint music was ethereal and orchestral. "High-end, hi-NRG," said Carroll about the early 1980s Euro disco with diva vocals he heard there. The Saint was spectacle, with its awe-inspiring planetarium. Speakers at the Saint were aimed directly at the dancers, creating a smooth, all-enveloping sound at around 146 decibels in the center. (A symphony orchestra generates 100 decibels.)

Like Carroll, Fort Lauderdale, Florida-based Leslie is also cosmopolitan and a survivor. He has worked at all kinds of clubs, gay and straight, at the service of the dancers on the floor. He went to Florida in the early 1980s to take a job as DJ Bobby Viteritti's light man at Poop Deck and Tangerine. He credits Viteritti as a first mentor who most influenced his sound. From there he met the owners of the Sandpiper on Fire Island and got a summer job there as a waiter in 1975. He was promoted to bartender, and then he asked the management if he could DJ. Satisfying the discriminating music industry professionals who spent summer weekends there was demanding. After dancing to reel-to-reel tapes made by the great New York City DJs, in 1976 Leslie took a chance as the first live Sandpiper DJ. The record companies would bring new imprints to try out on the vacationing crowd. If the gay crowd was sophisticated, it was also sympathetic to the new DJ's efforts. On his Saturday nights off, Leslie went into the city to dance at his favorite club, 12 West. The acoustical wood ceiling and wood, carpeted banquettes trapped the sound, resulting in "a magnificent tonal effect . . . The whole club acted like a giant horn." As a full-time DJ, he

DJ Robbie Leslie working at the Palladium in 1980. (Robbie Leslie)

was eligible to join Weinstien's Record Pool. By the time the Sandpiper closed on Halloween 1979, he was guesting at 12 West. His workweek included Underground Friday, Studio Thursday and Sunday. He also worked at Ice Palace, Palladium, and Red Parrot. Leslie rotated regularly with other DJs at the Saint from Christmas 1980 until 1986, when he returned to Florida. So many dancers succumbed to AIDS and drugs; the holes in the crowd were difficult for business and for sensitive souls.

Leslie's gay anthems at the Saint included Marlena Shaw's "Touch Me In The Morning," Beautiful Bend's "That's The Meaning," Cut Glass's "Without Your Love," Candi Staton's "When You Wake Up Tomorrow," and Jimmy Ruffin's "Hold On To My Love." Hundreds of speakers and innovative sound technology helped make the Saint experience feel celestial or heavenly. Dancers at the last, 48-hour marathon farewell party remember Leslie spinning "Hold On To My Love" as a great balloon descended from the dome into his outstretched hands.

Leslie is one of the few surviving DJs forever associated with the ethereal Saint era sound: a seamless blend of disco anthems, sentimental favorites, and esoterica including 1980s electronic European imports, love songs by disco divas, classic and orchestral disco music. When

Grace Jones, September 21, 1978. (Photo by Allan Tannenbaum)

disco fell out of favor, he had to reach out to independent artists like Pamala Stanley for "Come Out Of Hiding," Canadian, English, and Italian imports. He broke Viola Wills' "If You Could Read My Mind" and The Passengers' "Hot Leather." He introduced Miquel Brown and Evelyn Thomas, and then hi-NRG. His music changed with the crowd and with the times. "As long as there are dancehalls, I think there is a place for me," he said. He does not say to himself, "This is a great record and I know it is. I'm going to make them like it. That's not me and it never was" (Leslie 2010).

Finally, the DJ designed programs of "morning music" or "sleaze music" for a soft landing. This, said Leslie, was the time to shine for the most devoted dancers. He would play classical music at the end. Some would arrive then, just to hear that set.

Bobby Viteritti was DJ at the San Francisco Trocadero. He is best known for his morning music. Viteritti started in Florida at the Lower Deck Disco underneath the Poop Deck Restaurant at the Marlin Hotel in Fort Lauderdale. In the winter of 1977, however, antigay Anita Bryant brought unwanted and unfriendly attention to the clubs. Eyewitness News was outside capturing the nightlife that Bryant found so immoral. Grace Jones made a special appearance at the club and supported the crowd against Bryant's homophobia. She spoke out, diverging from her aptly chosen cover of the song "Tomorrow, Tomorrow" from the musical *Annie*.

> I'm gonna feel better tomorrow. I'm gonna feel even better tomorrow, especially, because what I'd like to do is make sure we get rid of . . . Anita Bryant tomorrow, that's for sure. . . . I mean really, it's a bit too much today already!
>
> . . . Good to be here. I love you. I love Florida. I don't understand how a bitch like that can be from Florida! It's not possible. You all are so beautiful! (Jones 1977)

Gay club patrons would never forget Jones's support. But despite her uplifting performance, many objected to the spotlight and stayed home. The economy was sinking also. Viteritti moved west in 1977 after seeing an ad for the huge San Francisco Trocadero Transfer. He brought his remix of a Donna Summer song, and it was playing when he met Troc owner Dick Collier. Collier hired him for a Halloween night Black Party. He at first had trouble. The crowd was used to DJ Gary Tighe, and Tighe's light man did not like Viteritti either. After a struggle, he won hearts. Bringing in Billy Langenheim to do lighting helped. They made a great team. Viteritti introduced Euro-disco diva Amanda Lear's "Follow Me" one night when he ran out of records. "It was designed for the interior of the Trocadero—that time and space," he said in an interview for the Web site DiscoMusic.com (Lopez 2002). The import, which had been out for a while, became a Troc anthem and staple. Lear's lyrics propose a Faustian exchange between music and dancer. Viteritti remixed it several times to keep it fresh for his audience.

Viteritti and DJ Gary Tighe tried to outdo each other at the Troc, but Viteritti had an uncommon talent. He played R&B, Latin, jazzy, and rockish music, emphasizing the midrange. He started out the evening with quick mixes, upbeat, traditional disco sets, and pretty songs like "First Love." Later, he would throw on some electronic music at the same tempo and confuse the crowd by alternating "real nelly, then butch, bomp—bomp—bomp." He would then bring the music down with a dark, twisted "popper" set of "obscure stuff" to "get [the dancers] all in the same headspace." In the dawn hours he would wind down with sleaze, for example, the 1974 Lamont Dozier song "Take Off Your Make Up." Viteritti would play this gay, cult, after-hours song for the few "hard-corettes" still on the premises. "Everyone sweats, everyone looks awful." But no one wanted to leave. An encore might start with "Relight My Fire." Morning dancers might hear "La Vie En Rose" or "Hot Butterfly." Since the proprietors only wanted to hire one DJ in those days, cocaine was a handy performance enhancer for the DJ (and dancers) who had to keep up his or her energy for the long stretch.

Viteritti won the Billboard National DJ of the Year in 1979 and 1980. He was able to create drama and tell stories with his music. He created the communal spirit, the "cultish, dance-family feeling." He was particular about the kinds of music he would play—no ballads or bubble gum, and he did not take requests. He preferred particular crowds and venues over others, and vice versa. His light strings did not appeal to leather and butch types. Some objected to the way he could manipulate the mood. He liked to disorient the audience by seamlessly switching songs in the break so that they did not know what they were hearing. He also wanted to control the live shows by telling the performers what songs to sing. "I felt like God up there" (Lopez 2002).

When crystal meth took over as the drug of choice, the hi-NRG music was frantic, 130–140 bpm. The demand for endless, driving, peak music increased. "I wasn't tapping my feet anymore," he recalled (Viteritti 2010). The life and the drugs took a toll on Viteritti, and he moved to New York City in 1986; but after a break of over 20 years, he is back, clean and sober, satisfying twenty-first-century fans. To dancers worldwide, this DJ reigned through the Troc's golden age. Leslie learned about presentation and theatrics from him and called him "a master not only of the mix, but of the entire environment of a dancer's experience" (Lopez 2002).

San Francisco Sound

Viteritti's performance was important to the developing San Francisco sound. In *Tribal Rites*, DJ Casey Jones describes the music's peaks and emotional swells and the elaborate planning and pacing of the evening.

Producer Patrick Cowley created the yang in San Francisco hi-NRG, the pounding, mechanical sound in the gay dance clubs. The Yin was the sensual black R&B divas like Donna Summer and Gloria Gaynor, singing of suppression. The gay community could relate. "I Will Survive" became an anthem on the dance floor. Bill Motley and John Hedges created the first essentially gay music labels Moby Dick and Megatone, respectively. Moby Dick recorded Ashford & Simpson's "Remember Me." Megatone recorded Sylvester.

Sylvester, having lived abroad, brought back strains of Euro disco that fed San Francisco sound, along with his high falsetto and his transsexual presence. Cowley created synthesizer layering on the most famous Sylvester song and gay anthem "You Make Me Feel (Mighty Real)." Sylvester's rapturous song is a "second tear." Released in 1978, it is a perpetual celebration. His scintillating, quasi-Motown voice is soft, as if he is opening a present or divulging a secret. The song's driving, insistent, up-beat reiterates that, in fact, they *were* out there on the dance floor, where gay men have "come out." There, at least, their love was real, sanctioned. A decade after Stonewall, the gay man's invisibility was such that realness still felt like a dream. "I feel real when you touch me."

Peter Shapiro called the song "epochal . . . the cornerstone of gay disco," and "the genesis of hi-NRG" in his book *Turn the Beat Around*. But he points out that with the emergence of hi-NRG, "Latin flair was banished." This homogenized the look of the dancing in gay San Francisco clubs. Cowley also gave "Dance (Disco Heat)" his treatment. It peaked at number 20 on the Hot 100 chart. He then produced Sylvester's *Stars* album. With only four songs, *Stars* "summed up the entire disco experience" (P. Shapiro 2005, 78). Cowley's futuristic 1981 song "Menergy" features Sylvester's high-strung vocals, at once

urgent and cool. "Menergy" defines San Francisco sound. Its clinical
hi-NRG coincided with the upsurge in crystal meth usage in gay clubs.
Cowley died of AIDS the next year.

Sylvester was an original. He made all of his costumes and gave an
act. Sylvester straddled opposite sects of the gay community—clones
and queens. He wore outrageous costumes, reinventing himself in
drag or in casual t-shirt and jeans (clone wear). While performing in
1977 and 1978 at the Elephant Walk bar on Eighteenth and Castro, people would gather outside to hear his covers of Ashford & Simpson's
"Over and Over," Patti LaBelle's "You Are My Friend," or Diana
Ross's "Love Hangover." He celebrated and identified with black
blues women, channeling Lena Horne, Josephine Baker, Ethel Waters,
and Bessie Smith. Indeed, the two extra-large black women Wash and
Rhodes backed him. Sylvester felt perfectly comfortable in his skin.
With his falsetto voice and his "drag-fabulousness . . . he became
San Francisco's own disco-soul-diva" (Gamson 2008, 3). Each adoring
individual, clone or queen, felt that Sylvester was addressing him personally. His shamelessness was a model for *all* the gay men who had
flocked to San Francisco to come out. He was the performer of choice
and the voice of gay pride events and disco events (which are interre-
lated).

Like disco itself, Sylvester got big. He called *Stars* his "first completely disco album," and then added that it would probably be his
last. But instead of abandoning *Stars* fans, he got on the disco bandwagon when Marty Blecman signed him to Megatone. With "Do You
Wanna Funk?" they *set out* to make dance music. Cowley wrote the
music, and Sylvester wrote the lyrics.

In the mid-1980s, nearing 40, he had moved on artistically. He told
David Diebold, "I'm not a gay act anymore." He recovered his early
love for gospel and blues in a performance at Trocadero. Sylvester died
of AIDS not long after that in December 1988. His songs had buoyed
disco-era protest and pride. His call to action was a call to dance.

Gamson suggests that Sylvester's blackness made him approach-
able by the divergent groups. If he is not better remembered today, it
is perhaps because of his chameleon-like onstage presence. The mainstream masses did not know what to make of the gay, black hero, back
in the day. However, in 2005, he was one of three artists inducted into
the Dance Music Hall of Fame.

Chic

On the East Coast, back in 1972, New York guitarist Nile Rodgers was working on Sesame Street and playing with the likes of Aretha Franklin at the Apollo at night. He met bass player Bernard Edwards in 1977, and they fronted Chic, complemented by vocalists Norma Jean Wright and Alfa Anderson and drummer Tony Thompson. Their debut album *Chic* had a number six hit, "Dance, Dance, Dance," and a number one hit, the 10-minute long "Everybody Dance." They dressed in professional attire, to match their aspirations, and mirrored the black urban professionals who were in their audiences. Nevertheless, when Grace Jones invited them to join her at Studio 54, they were turned away at the door. Thus begins the now well-known tale of their next hit, "Le Freak." They walked a few blocks to their studio where they let off steam about the ironic rejection. "Le Freak" is a tongue-in-cheek celebration of downtrodden outcasts' capacity for elevation. The song gives release in dance to the masses who could remember having been, at any time, treated like second-class citizens. Their 1979 production *We Are Family* with Sister Sledge reached R&B number one and number two on the pop charts. Their hits had massive appeal. Not only that, Rodgers is "quite possibly the greatest rhythm guitar player ever," writes Peter Shapiro. "Thompson's punishing, metronomic, [drums] practically bludgeoned you into submission on the dance floor" (P. Shapiro 2005, 163, 167).

Michael Jackson

Michael Jackson has an odd relationship with disco, as does James Brown, Madonna, or superstardom itself. Brown and Jackson are iconoclastic legendary dancers and recording artists of the disco era. They made dance music with a repetitive, consistent beat and simple lyrics that are echoes of the beat and imperatives to dance, love, or be kind. But superstardom conflicted with disco's deauthorization, where the studio production, the DJ and, ultimately, social dancers were the stars. Brown's commands to "Get up" and "Get down" were opposite to McCoy's gentle lyricism. But Jackson, updating Brown's art of movement and music, put in the sugar. Jackson was pure pop. Both crossed over, performing largely for white audiences. After "Say It Loud," Brown had the attention of blacks and black men, especially. Jackson

Michael Jackson. (Photofest)

reached out to his black brethren in chummy music videos that addressed us-and-them issues. But Jackson was all about togetherness between races, ages, and genders. His *Destiny* and *Triumph* albums had an image of the peacock on the cover, signifying their wish to "integrate all races through music," Michael and Jackie Jackson wrote in a liner note. As difficult as it was for the child star to emerge as an adult, his public had as much trouble accepting the adult who was emerging. Unlike many other child stars, his art continued to grow, change, and flourish in the public eye.

One can chart his growth in the many promotional music videos he made, and his television appearances, including a Pepsi commercial (which many fans used as proof that he had sold out). He was always the star and front man-child of The Jackson Five. He still looks like a child in a "Billie Jean" music video in which he steps on squares of light and executes his most famous pose. Balanced on the points of his wing tips, his s-shaped form hovers over the floor. In this surreptitious but immaculate Romeo and Juliet story, he is a boy approaching manhood. He climbs into her window and into her bed. (We never actually see her.) Then he is gone. The new video technology allowed Michael to stand *en pointe* for a few seconds and to disappear from the fantasy quicker than you can say "Nijinsky."

Elvis takes a similar pose in the 1957 movie musical *Jailhouse Rock*, but he is sneakered and twisted, out-of-the-box. Jackson's pose is anything but cute and playful. He had surely seen Jeffrey Daniel, the West Coast street dancer and Shalamar member, on *Soul Train*. Daniel was playing up the slides and robotic breaks in mime and tap dances. Yet Jackson came to own the moves, over the years. On the King of Pop, it was the famous moonwalk. He performed the moves to "Dancing Machine" on Merv Griffin in 1974 (Popper 2009).

In 1978, Jackson played the Scarecrow in *The Wiz*. There he met the show's musical supervisor and producer Quincy Jones, who produced Jackson's *Off the Wall* the next year. It sold five million copies in the United States. Four songs were in Top 10. Jones also produced *Thriller* in 1982, which had seven Top 10 songs and replaced *Saturday Night Fever* as the all-time, best-selling album.

Berry Gordy invited the Jacksons, who had reunited for the event, to the 1983, televised Motown 25th anniversary celebration. The occasion prompted Michael's breakthrough performance of his evolved "Billie Jean" solo, wearing his one white glove, a fedora (which he promptly cast away), a black sequined jacket and black pants, a silver shirt, glittery white socks, and dress loafers. One hand, then the other goes into his pocket while he pumps his pelvis. One leg whips out to the front and swipes at the fourth wall, in a single beat. The toe-end of his fancy, shiny black shoes, or both of them somehow, smash imaginary insects or burning embers into the floor. Twice, he seems to float backward in his moonwalk, to squeals from the audience. It is this slippery move that brings delight. When he high-steps in an excited, equine, run-in-place, that, too, excites the audience. His bent knees are together and his feet apart when he rests, facing forward, for a split second, like a sly fox, on his toes in the iconic s-pose. It is a kind of bow. Fred Astaire complimented him on his routine. "You knocked them on their asses out there, kid. You're an angry dancer, there's rage in your feet" (Martin 1995, 782).

After a successful decade or more of pop stardom, the Jacksons went on a last Victory Tour. According to the British music critic Gavin Martin, to save face, they made a charity event of it. He donated his share, $5 million. For whatever reason, much of the rest of Michael's performing career was outward looking. The proceeds from his next *We Are The World* in 1984 went to USA for Africa.

Jackson's stardom had peaked, and he began to disappoint. Yet, the 1987 *Bad* had five number one singles on it. Jackson toured to 15 countries and gave 123 concerts that year, donating tickets and profits to charities. He bought the ranch in Los Oliveros in 1988 and called it Neverland. It had a zoo, a movie theater, a roller coaster, and other children's entertainment. But charges of molestation followed. And MJ, in his public statements, did not do enough to set people's minds at ease. A jury found him innocent, but he never recovered from the rumors and allegations.

Jackson was looking for family, the way gay dancers on the floor were. He allied himself with women and children, having grown up in a family that worked together, with a strict and menacing father who had terrorized him. He and his siblings had played childish pranks including throwing water balloons out the window. As the Peter Pan figure that was real and age 44 in 2002, he shocked the world with one brief gesture: he dangled a small bundle out a Berlin hotel window. It appeared to be his infant with a towel over its head.

His music was not so sweet anymore. *Dangerous* was true to its name. Said Martin, "Dangerous is a huge, sprawling work packed with overweening kitsch, dumb ugly metal, yahoo rousing rockers, hard raps, that break his voice into epileptic fits, growls, yelps" (Martin, 784). He did donate all the profits from the *Dangerous* tour to his Pepsi-sponsored Heal the World Foundation. He had moved on from the Quincy Jones sound. Fans were critical of his increasingly bizarre behavior. He was spending extravagantly, addicted to prescription drugs, and the subject of mockery. It appeared that he was reinventing himself as a whiter Diana Ross. He had once lived with Ross; she had taken him under her wing. When pressed, he attributed the bleached look to vitiligo, but he was not forthcoming with any apologies for his surgically altered features and ghostlike appearance. Nevertheless, such fame leads to a feeling of ownership, and the public deeply resented his changing face. Michael retreated after the abuse allegation, even though the jury found him innocent. He lived his last years reclusively on an island in Bahrain.

He had bills to pay, and he was pushing himself to make a comeback. Jackson was in rehearsal for a London debut when he died of an overdose of pills in 2009. The world mourned what seemed a sudden death; few knew of his frail physical condition. The view from across the pond in *The Faber Book of Pop*, "A cursory look at the path travelled by any black American celebrity of this century . . . shows that they undertake a strange, often perilous journey" (Martin 1993).

A public still reeling from Jackson's recent death can enjoy mountains of documentation about the life of the star, who Elizabeth Taylor named "King of Pop" in 1989. Whatever problems we had with him, we mourn the tragic end of this most magnificent dancer.

Videos are available at the click of the mouse (VH1 n.d.), and several are disco. "Rock With You" is a bonus track from *Bad* (1987). Jackson wears a sparkly sequined jumpsuit, and lights pinwheel in the background. He grooves with the microphone in the spotlight. He wants to rock the night away with you.

"Remember the Time" (a performance of the song from *Dangerous*, 1991) has a disco, camp sensibility. A fire-eater and a snake charmer come before Eddie Murphy and supermodel Iman as a Nefertiti character. They are not amused and order the performers' heads chopped off. Jackson appears in a black cloak, as a cool contender. He spreads a handful of nails on the floor and then walks on them, showing no pain. He then sinks through a circular patch of quicksand that replaces the nails. He rises up swaddled in shimmering gold, as his song jogs Nefertiti's memories of their times on the beach and at the bar. She falls for him as he spins in a gauzy skirt with black leather pants underneath. But Murphy re-enters and some spear-wielding men are aiming for Jackson, who shrinks into a spray of glitter. Magical, yet it is typically nightmarish.

In the 1978 "Blame It On The Boogie," the Jacksons get into the disco spirit that their Motown music had helped bring about. This is a danceable ballad by Mike Jackson (no relation) about a girl he gives up on because she won't stop dancing. The performer, on his Destiny Tour, grinds his toe into the ground while his heel switches back and forth. He raises his knees alternately, running in place with his head high. With knees bent, he opens and closes his feet in a gravity-defying cross between a slide and a small jump. The lyrics explain the supernatural feat. The devil has him in a trance.

The disco hit "Don't Stop Till You Get Enough" is from the Jackson album *HIStory Past, Present, and Future.* Jackson performs it live on the Triumph tour, in tux and bow tie. He does his slip-sliding dance in solo, transporting us with his infectious jouissance. He runs and jumps across the stage and into the aisles with the seemingly bound-less energy of his teenage youth. By 1979, the song was number one. Michael wrote it himself. His mother objected to its sexual references. He performs in bunched, sparkly white socks, patent leather shoes, and a corsage. He says in an after talk, "As long as the people enjoy it, I'll always be happy."

4

Dance the Night Away

The dance floor was an arena for coming out in every way, and all ways, in the 1970s. Dancing gave voice to young people who may have been shy and inhibited in verbal conversation but found they could speak with their bodies. Dancing, in every era, is an expression of joining with the music, with a partner, and with a community of dancers on the floor. These three levels of enjoyment came together with an exuberance that defined the disco era. Self-expression was a new mainstream means, but the end involved ideals of unity.

Freestyle dancing was the kinetic activity for the me generation. "Each person finds his own means of expression within the driving magic of Disco . . . " said Jena Lauren in her 1979 book *Disco*. Dancing singly was newly fashionable in the 1960s, and then the subsequent coming together on 1970s dance floors had to be accomplished in a new way. Lauren called dancing "the national evening sport" appealing to people from all walks of life. Forty of the top 100 hits were disco songs in 1978. By then, the word disco referred to the discotheque, the music, and the dances (Lauren 1979).

Jerolyn Ann Nentl, in her 1980 *Disco Dancing*, wrote that disco dancing made you feel like a star if you were good. Dancers made up a new dance every time they stepped out on the floor. They could sense each other's turns. They forgot their troubles. Nentl implies that disco dancing came from France, along with the discotheque. In particular, she names a 1960s Parisian disco partner dance called "wheeling." A convergence of influences—jazz, African, Latin, ballroom, and rock—spurred the disco phenomenon. Latino and black dancers inspired the new styles. Haight-Ashbury hippie culture with its bright lights and costumes contributed. Castro gay culture was then celebrating new visibility and influence. The style is "glamorous, free and easy, and pure fantasy . . . Tony [Manero]'s style became today's disco style." Movements are large, as if the dancer is drawing in space with outstretched arms and legs. "They glide across the floor letting each step or turn melt into the next one. . . . The disco look is a strut that says 'Look at ME. I'm a star' " (Nentl 1980).

Dance studios blossomed as people in urban cities and suburbs wanted to join in. The infectious music heard on the radio or in the local bar or disco, with its heavy bass beat, was a motivator. John Travolta's Tony Manero was a magnetic role model for people seeking opportunities to better themselves. The message of *Saturday Night Fever* is that dance helped him do this. He elicited enormous empathy and widespread identification. To moviegoers, self-improvement seemed possible through dance.

Musical performers modeled steps. Concertgoers no longer wanted to stand or sit on the sidelines and listen. The me generation was very proactive. Yet, the feeling of being entranced, out-of-control and even out-of-body, was the aim—meanwhile, looking good. Practice and skill resulted in comfort and attractiveness. If one of the aims of disco dancing was community with another, or many, then attraction was a means.

Feeling free and letting go through disco dancing was the way to fulfill the era's positive valuation of fitness, physicality, sexuality, and self-awareness. "Stand as tall as you can and breathe naturally. Lift the ribcage and stretch the body upward keeping the shoulders relaxed and comfortably pulled down and back," says Lauren.

Developing one's own style was important, but dancers could learn the basics in studios, books, and dance shows, and from others on the floor. Rocking and strutting with alternating or parallel arms characterize the basic disco step. Tap and step, no hips. The body is vertical, and the arms and hands are used to add expression and style, as in ballet and other dance forms.

Lauren, from Los Angeles, adds posing to her disco dance repertoire. Moving the body in freeze-frame increments, she instructs her readers to hold the pose for 2–8 counts. Lauren's posing lessons recall ball and runway culture and Madonna's later music video, "Vogue."

Lauren calls this vogue-like communication "body language." For John Travolta, some of his models, and his many imitators, that included pointing the index finger while extending the right arm at about 2:00. This move can be interpreted as prideful, imperative, or assertive. In club language, circling the index finger in a small circle overhead means, "let's go." A raised arm in the dance floor crowd, with the thumb up or down, will tell the DJ to raise or lower the volume. Tony Manero twaddles his forearms. In ballet, this gesture is an invitation to dance. In disco, it has the same meaning. In a cool, teasing, avoidant move, the hands are pushed downward and forward, as if to distance the partner or resist his/her invitation. The dancer is playing hard to get. At the same time, it is a come-on.

Karen Lustgarten had studied ballet and jazz. In her twenties, she observed freestyle dancing in San Francisco clubs and dance bars. In the early 1970s, she started recording her observations and breaking down the steps. Fast and slow were the two modes, dictated by the songs. The new orchestral music by Tavares and passion-filled vocals by Gloria Gaynor, for example, called for movement that was abstract and fluid. She observed people expressing the music through their movement in that way. Seeing a need and a market for formal instruction, she held lessons in her basement studio; a package of four cost $10. So many signed on that she raised the price to $12 and moved to the newly opened Dance Your Ass Off disco (Lustgarten 2009).

One or two months later, in January 1976, Lustgarten's classes numbered 200 or more. She wrote teacher's manuals and trained 10 in The Lustgarten Technique. Two nights a week, before official opening time, she held separate beginning and advanced classes. She and DJ Marc Richardson wrote lesson plans and choreographed the class. They engaged in a kind of sign language communication, synchronizing the music and dance.

Lustgarten's fast dances have names like Loose Booty and Rock Steady in *The Complete Guide to Disco Dancing* she published in 1978. It is divided into 10 freestyle lessons, line Hustle dances, and partner Hustle dances, in succession. She visited New York to see partner Hustle dancing. "People thought disco was hustle. All three made it fun," she said (Lustgarten 2009).

There were ever-proliferating options for single dancers at West Coast parties. Instructors taught the Bus Stop and the line Hustle or Continental Walk. In the Bus Stop, step forward and the feet meet with

Karen Lustgarten is pictured on the disco music stamp, one of fifteen 1970s stamps issued in the USPS 1999 series "Celebrate the Century." Lustgarten wrote in the accompanying description, "Some Americans caught disco fever." (Copyright United States Postal Service)

a rocking motion. Repeat with deeper rocking on bent knees. Two 90-degree turns bring you to the original front-facing position. The line Hustle is for two or more. Take four steps back and four forward. Step to the right and bring the left foot to meet it. Then step to the left and bring the right foot there. Jump forward, jump back, and click the heels. Pivot in a quarter turn, and kick to each side. Endless variations of these basic line dances provided endless fun on the dance floor. They also crowded out anyone trying to dance with a partner.

West Coast dancers saw the New York Hustle when it caught the eye of Cuban-born San Franciscoan, TV producer Ron Bermudez. After Bermudez saw *Saturday Night Fever*, he went to New York. He video-taped Floyd Chisholm, Nelly Cotto, Eddie Vega, and Lourdes Jones performing. The production was a hit on a California cable access channel in 1978. But many found it too difficult to learn just by watching and copying moves. West Coast teachers helped spread Hustle's migration.

West Coast "Touch" Dances

Lauren observed a return to touch dancing and the delight of learning to second-guess your partner. The leader begins all touch dances stepping or tapping with the left foot. The follower, in opposition, begins with the right foot.

The man travels little, while guiding the woman. She travels side to side facing him. If travelling to the right, she pivots right; if travelling left, she pivots left. The arms are relaxed and move in large circular patterns. The man clasps the woman's right hand with his left. Dancing side by side, their arms swing up and down in a large circle. They take several steps forward and then a step and quarter turn to face each other. Turns are a way of adding musicality, personality, and fun to basic partner or Hustle steps. Lauren cites four turning styles: inside and outside, cage turn, sweetheart turn, and windmill turn (the latter two with double handhold).

Disco Swing begins with a small and controlled tap of the toe, close to the heel of the opposite foot. The partners step out to the same side. They swing from side to side while dancing fast triple steps. The follower's hand is on the leader's shoulder, and he rests his hand on her back. They can face each other or dance in an open position.

Roy Madrid writes in his 1978 *Disco . . . You Should Be Dancing* that Disco Swing is the easiest of the partner dances. The feet alternate and dancers step on the ball of the foot. The center of gravity is in their chest area. Do not grab too tight, he advises, so that her hand can pivot inside his during turns. After two sets of basic steps, he nudges her to one side, into a turn. He loosely clasps her hand in his, above her head, while she turns under the bridge. The man moves around the woman, facilitating her turns. He can then turn under her bridge 180 degrees.

Madrid was billed as a competition disco dancer, teacher of many Hollywood stars, and "King of Disco Dancers" in an ad for mini-classes at The Broadway, an L.A. department store. Disco fashion shows followed each lesson. He and his dancers demonstrated the latest steps to the rich and famous at socialites' disco parties and dinners. One cocktail party written up in the *Los Angeles Times* style section called him a "special consultant for *Saturday Night Fever*, the film that brought disco to the LA social scene" (J. Jacobs 1978). "Saturdays at Robinson's" featured a *Charlie's Angels* look-alike contest and a dance contest. The 1978 ad promised winners one free lesson with "LA's leading disco dance instructor, Roy Madrid." He taught Latin Hustle, New York Hustle, and Disco Swing with another disco champion, Nicholas Rey, at Aisha Ali Studio in Culver City.

Roy Madrid's Partner Dances:

STEPS: stomp, tap, pivot, touch (a meeting of the feet).

POSITIONS: facing, cradle, crossed, facing (final).

Facing: hands clasped in center with the woman's palms down and the
man's facing up. He is inviting her to dance with his upturned
palms. She accepts by inserting hers into his open palms. His feet
are together, and he lets the woman approach him.

Cradle position: Man raises his left hand. Lady turns clockwise underneath. They end side-by-side, facing the same direction, with his
arm crossing in front of her, as if to rock or cradle her.

Crossed position: They cross their arms in the center with the left arm
always on top.

Final (facing) position: Man's hand is on her back. Hers is on his
shoulder.

Each dance has its own turning variation, Madrid wrote. Dips can
be added. (The man dips or drops his partner into a backbend; his
arm at the small of her back leverages her weight.) Lauren and Madrid
taught a Tango 500, or Tango Hustle, with dips. The woman can raise a
leg while leaning back. The head turns in the direction of their
weighted steps to the side, as in ballroom Tango. Latin Hustle "allows
couples to dance intimately to fast music." Madrid's Latin Hustle is
smooth and fluid and with the hands always connected. The dancers
take seven steps in six counts, with an extra walking step at the end.

In his jokey book, Madrid lays out a prescriptive, macho style. He
cites a "desirable disco consciousness." In other words, a cool, hard-to-
get attitude will make you desirable. "The successful disco dancer is
cool and composed." His suggestions require real work. He advocates
attention to erect posture, confidence, and regular practice. The couple
is a team, he says, and they communicate with body language. The
leader must have strong arms and "get a grip on himself." The follower
mirrors the leader. Steps should be small (Madrid 1978).

Despite Bermudez's auspicious introduction, as the Hustle crossed
the country from East to West, teachers and dancers defined Latin,
New York, and street Hustle differently. Some called the Hustle from

New York's El Barrio, the New York Hustle. The trend was toward deracination. In contrast, New York Hustle pros formed a network. They set guidelines. Basically, the first tap or step is preparatory. It propels the dancer forward into the routine. Hustle is a walking dance. The count is simply & 1-2-3.

The Looks

With disco dancing came dressy clothes. Three-piece white suits, gold neck chains, and fitted black shirts of silky or satiny material showed off the male dancer's build. Lauren reports, "Disco fashions from France include triple-pleated pants and loosely bloused shirts." She suggests bodysuits worn with wrap skirts that open at the hip and dancewear made of Milliskin that shimmers under the disco lights— shiny, clingy, slinky, sexy—pants that tie around the ankle or dresses with full skirts that flare while twirling. Jazz and ballroom-dance shoes finish the look.

"Dusts are what's happening in disco make-up." These loose powders in shimmering colors "look terrific under lights. You can dust anything and everything." Disco dancers used flowers, combs, barrettes, braids, or ponytails to keep the hair off the face. Others used their long and flowing hair as part of their dance or wore it short and chic. The variable hairstyles were part of a disco dancer's individuality. Nentl says the natural look is out. Along with slim body-hugging shirts and pants, or swirling skirts, women wore lots of mascara to maximize the visual spectacle of their movement in the theatrical lighting. Some created individual solutions beyond the stereotypical.

If disco dancing offered the sense of remaking oneself, costume was all-important. This was especially evident in the gay disco world. Consider Sylvester as he dressed for chosen fantasies and modeled star quality for every disco dancer. Gay dancers donned freaky styles and uniforms of the motorcyclist, sailor, correction officer, nurse, and confabulations thereof. In the 1977 Harper's article *Disco*, Helgesen suggests that who you are is baggage and you can travel light by dropping your identity. She introduces Rene, a 21-year-old make-up artist who went out dancing four nights a week for eight years. He preferred the most fancy places where he could wear the most outrageous clothes.

For celebutantes, club kids, and vogueing runway performers, dance was an integral part of their remaking. The latter group may take their dance to choreographed excellence. Club dancers wanted to be seen and to perform. For some, social dancing led to artistic aspirations. Dancers went out to see the new steps, learn, and excel. Dancing remade them.

Fashions of the day inspired the looks that Tony Manero made popular in the movie *Saturday Night Fever*. John Travolta wanted to wear a black suit but settled on white for visibility. *Saturday Night Fever* was two months behind the *Roseland* premiere. In that film, Floyd Chisholm also wears a white suit. In a 1973 *Soul Train* episode, a dancer wears a white suit and bow tie. The Soul Train Dancers would find costumes in vintage clothing stores for Gatsby, Gangster, and Locker looks. Their creativity set trends.

Whatever the source, the double image—two 1977 disco dancing film stars wearing white suits, the black Chisholm and the white Travolta—had to have bolstered the popularity of the iconic look, for people of all races. The male, Brooklyn dancers who frequented Odyssey (in real life) wore suits with flared pants and cheap, body-hugging shirts in prints or a solid color. One such dancer, the possible prototype for Vincent, greeted Cohn in 1975 at the Odyssey door and vomited on him. He wore crimson pants and had a cool, star-quality presence. Girls came in groups of three or four wearing Lycra body suits under skirts or tight jeans—and heels, of course.

Saint Dances

The repetitive beats of Saint music embodied desire. Submitting to those beats, gay club patrons could celebrate their identity. Before 1973, the medical model implied that homosexuals were suffering. When the Saint opened, it had only been six years since the American Psychological Association removed homosexuality from its list of disorders. Along with the repetitive, pounding beats, powerful, nurturing women's vocals guided the celebratory mood on the Saint dance floor.

Some disco songs invoke the female orgasm and autoerotic ecstasy with "endless cycles and plateaus." Patrons at the Saint could dance singly to orgasmic songs by Donna Summer, Gloria Gaynor, and others, completing a relationship with the performer. The dancers improvised expressions of jouissance. They might also dance with successive, multiple contacts to the DJ's spliced songs (Hughes 1993).

We can think of any social dance as a mating dance, and dancing at the Saint was no exception. Owner Bruce Mailman described the style of movement as implied (play) violence but not explicit sexuality. People were always stripped to the waist and looking at each other. They met on the dance floor, flirted, and touched. "It was a very primal, direct, and wild place," said Mailman (The Saint 2007).

At the Saint, the men were called clones because they dressed alike in Levi's 501 jeans, with a T-shirt in their back pocket and a color-coded bandana according to their sexual preferences. At Saint Black circuit parties, they wore leather. At White ones, the mood was lighter and happier (at first). The 501s were White. Everyone worked out at a gym, and the Saint was the place to show off a chiseled chest. Dancing was mostly freestyle, and arms were raised above in a sort of hailing to the musical performer. The body language read as sexual openness, a generosity of heart and soul, a vulnerability and trust in potential partners, and a lemming-like togetherness of the community of dancers. If the floor was crowded, dancers were close packed. Yet the range of movement was surprising, within the necessary verticality. It was a tribal experience, and individuals danced with the unifying music. Nevertheless, according to DJ Robbie Leslie, the men often danced in pairs or in small groups of three or four. Dancers soloed on the banquettes that ringed the floor.

When a clone removed his shirt, instead of sticking it in his back pocket, he might wave it around overhead, in a circular motion, like a lasso. He might also wave and rotate only his hand or index finger. The underlying urban cowboy aesthetic may have brought flagging, fanning, and variations thereof to club dance floors. Japanese fan dances also influenced.

Dancers graduated from shirts to translucent or reflective silk fans and flags. They flung voluminous, tie-dyed flags or translucent fans overhead in circle eight patterns, catching light from the rotating disco balls above. Their light-filled silks spread and disseminated pastel dots. They swish them low to the ground and then spiral them up and overhead. Dancers wield the fans and flags like paintbrushes or swords, depending on the mood. The flags are like wings, colorful butterfly wings, as the dancers swirl two as extensions of their arms. Manipulated in creative, empowering, and signal-like gestures, they recall Loie Fuller's art nouveau dances with light-filled silky fabrics. Fuller also extended her reach with wands. The Saint dancer became a

Flagger, 2009. (Ortiz)

sexually ambiguous form with these spinning, beating extensions, especially in the morning hours when the floor was uncrowded.

Flag and fan club dances require strength, stamina, rhythm, and co-ordination at the very least. Some dancers can elicit the ideal jouis-sance with their movement, within a limited floor area. An expert dancer can manipulate fans gyroscopically at various points along the outer, supporting sturdy sticks. It is a walking dance, like other freestyle, line, and partner dances of the disco era. Walking helps the dancer follow the beat of the music—thus, the dance's aptness for parades and pride marches.

A few women guests were allowed into the membership only, male Saint on Sundays after 1982, for example, women in the music industry like DJ Sharon White, and Canada, who learned to dance with fans and flags at Saint-at-Large parties held in the original Saint shell and elsewhere after the club closed.

Canada became adept at these new forms. The forceful whisk of her fan in figure eight patterns could be read as a flushing out of sadness and pain. The remembrance of all those who died is palpable in Saint-at-Large and in twenty-first-century Holy Spirit Dance Club parties. Her fan is not a delicate thing. At an April 2010 HSDC tea dance at Elmo's, when the fans were not acting smoothly, she dropped them to the floor and stomped on them to loosen up the wood spokes. She then took out two ribbon wands (foil streamers attached to the end of wooden sticks). They would be easier to handle. She flung them in similar, alternating figure eight patterns. HSDC dancers consider Canada the originator of this ribbon-wand club dance.

One HSDC member, a card-carrying former Saint member, recalled playing a percussion instrument and doing "K" bumps (1980s party drug) with a group sitting under the tree, the famous planetarium-sized, rotating light bank that rose toward the dome ceiling of the Saint. For many dancers, drugs fueled marathons back in the day. Survivors dancing at Elmo's in 2010 were celebrating life. They wore well-chosen, expressive t-shirts (those who were not in theme, infirmary costume). Big warning letters across the front of one spelled out "Don't Ask Me for Drugs."

Back in the day, said DJ Bobby Viteritti, dancers made fans by affixing silver or silky fabric onto the shorn ribs of cheap Chinatown paper fans. Then, beads added weight and reflective surface. Makers sewed weighted cords in places, to facilitate their thrust.

There is some disagreement as to whether the form began on the East or West Coast, at the Saint or San Francisco's Trocadero. Nevertheless, flagging and fanning evolved on regular Saint nights and at Saint Black, White, Red, and other special parties, at marathon dances that could go on for 20 hours, at long weekend circuit parties, and at parades and pageants.

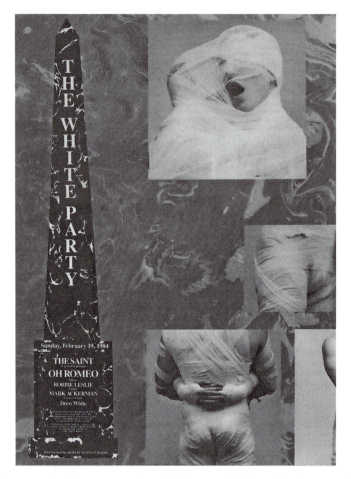

Saint White party poster, 1984, in the LGBT Center, NYC archive. Images from the series White Gauze, 1984. (Copyright The Robert Mapplethorpe Foundation. Courtesy Art + Commerce)

After AIDS diminished the Saint membership and the club closed, the Gay Men's Health Crisis mailing list created a national circuit for raising money and people who wanted to keep dancing. Women helped fill the ranks. White parties that started out as happy occasions for rebirth took on medical associations because of the many ill and dying from AIDS. In the late 1980s, we saw a gay cancer with no medication or strategy for its control. Someone wrote to complain about health risk at the Saint, and Mailman put up a sign saying, "The balcony was designed as a viewing platform—PLEASE USE IT THAT WAY" (Wandel n.d.).

South by Southwest

Viteritti started in Florida, making music for gay crowds at the Lower Deck under the Poop Deck and at the Marlin Beach Hotel in Fort Lauderdale in the mid-1970s. He saw gay dancers do the Hustle in bars until *Saturday Night Fever*, after which everyone stopped doing it. The gay crowds he played for had a great appreciation for the music, has a sense of rhythm, and loved to dance. Straight people with such musicality came to the gay bars. Cubans would drive up from Miami for the Lower Deck Sunday tea dances. Couples danced the Hustle together, or individuals roamed around with a Cha-Cha step, chatting with everyone, to Viteritti's program of disco (and other) songs. "I was user friendly," he said. After two years, the grandeur of the West called him.

At the Trocadero Transfer, music and dancing were of a piece. Viteritti kept his eye on the dancers without them knowing it. Around 2 a.m. to 4 a.m. they might all do a line Hustle called the Trocadero Shuffle. The floor was a concert of mood, music, and movement. For single dancers with tambourines and with fans, "It was like playing with yourself in your own space." At the end of the night, with the slower music and thinner crowd, the fans helped buoy the visually exciting atmosphere. Their silver or sparkly material reflected the light.

Viteritti's morning or sleaze music had Troc dancers walking around screaming and cheering. When the music picked up, they would be "doing that march, stamping do-*DEEE*-do ... do-*DEEE*-do," the whole room full of 200 or so buff, sweaty hard-corettes looking at each other. Fan dances enhanced their visual, kinetic, and auditory experience. Many used acid and Quaaludes to induce their hallucinogenic trip (Viteritti 2010).

Around the time Viteritti had had enough, he presciently said, "We don't have to dance for twelve hours and blow our brains out to have a good time" (Diebold 1986, 203). At this writing, he is once again working in New York City. He goes to 12-step meetings and says he has discovered coffee.

At Studio

Characters dressed up in order to get into Studio 54. In 1979, Sally Lippman was a 78-year-old former member of the Bar Association who loved to dance. Known as Disco Sally, photographers caught her in an ornate mask and dancing center stage. She was a Studio regular. So was the young roller-skating Rollerena who wore a Ginger Rogers–style gown. It was a time of free expression. Looking amazing or dressing in your fantasy, that was the ticket. Nude dancers in metallic body paint, and aerial dance acts—Warhol, Devine, Liz Taylor, Liza Minnelli, Martha Graham, Grace Jones, and Bianca Jagger—they were all spectacles greeting insiders. Well, the insiders were the spectacles. Entering on a white horse, Jagger could channel the archetypal heroine on her birthday night. Paparazzi photographer Ron Galella was not alone in saying that getting into Studio was his single-most important life goal. Inside the glass doors, the chosen were the new A-list stars of the evening. In the earlier hours, dancers did not touch very much. They learned steps from each other. "Then as it got late and things got sleazy, you hung on for dear life. You did not just dance with one person. You could dance with ten people if you wanted to" (Bromley 2008).

Lofty Dances

At David Mancuso's downtown Broadway Loft, there was no set program of music, but there was a beginning, a middle, and a reentry period. That, Mancuso said, was the most important (Ramos 2003). The crowd was mixed with a gay, black presence. They danced on their own, but dancers from different groups bonded. One dancer after another would jump into a ring and show his or her moves, fostering the sense of camaraderie. This came directly from street dancing, where many uptown corners had a dancer ringed with onlookers. Inside, dancers performed a continuing story in movement. They did breaking, hip-hop, and smooth walks. There were no hired performers, and dress was casual.

Archie Burnett told historian Sally Sommer that he began his club life as a Lofter. "It was my first experience in a very cool atmosphere . . . not too white, not too black, not too straight, not too gay, you know . . . truly cool." Dancers wore clothes that moved, baggy pants and t-shirts they could sweat in. They brought duffel bags with a change of clothes, towel, and powder. They might add flavors or colorful accessories that stood out (Sommers 2001, 77).

Mancuso's famously unexpected musical choices, like the little known (in 1972) Afro-Latin percussive group Manu Dibango, fueled the innovative, freestyle moves. Dancing at the Loft was serious business. Admission fees were nominal donations. Mancuso's no-nonsense, low-tech, nonprogram of music set the tone.

Trading Ballrooms

Ball culture fomented underground in 1970s co-opted Harlem spaces. The walks count among dance styles of the day. The House of Extravaganza and the House of Omni are two of about twenty families or Houses meeting in uptown venues during the disco era. The names played on designer fashion institutions like Vogue and Chanel. Each House had a Mother, a Father, and Children (younger, newer, or less-respected dancers on the floor). The balls functioned as surrogate families for gay teens.

Kevin Omni, father of the House of Omni and the foremost speaker on ball culture, first started going to the balls in 1979. He described the early presentations as "very Las Vegas showgirl" and cabaret style. "Jail queens" from Rikers Island, New York, invented vogue or vogueing in the 1970s, and ball walkers developed the style—freeze-frame poses, runway-style walks, and expressive, gesticulating arms and hands (Kevin Ultra Omni 1992).

Participants carefully assembled their looks and then competed in high fashion and fantasy costumes to qualify in a category, for example, butch queen, male, executive, opulence, military, or sex siren. They walked down a central, longitudinal, runway-like performing area (in the documentary *Paris Is Burning*). Judges looked for realness within the various categories. That is, how well did the contestant accomplish the transformation? Finally, performers representing their Houses competed. They vied for prizes, cash, trophies, and moments of stardom. Walkers could achieve topmost, legendary status in their lifetime. Three grand prize wins made them legends.

Transgender performers in the Harlem ballrooms surely realized the disco notion of remaking the self. Dances, looks, and spoken language from ball culture crossed over into other social dance arenas. For example, ball words and concepts like realness, and throwing shade (directing an undermining gesture toward a competitor), were applicable in larger dance circles. In the mid-1970s, one saw fan dances and Afro-centric vogueing in nightclubs and in gay and mixed gatherings. Dancers who enjoyed the balls also danced in clubs, performed in concerts, and competed in other genres. For example, the *Paris Is Burning* cast includes a drag performer in fur, with unmistakable dance authority. He is also a Hustle pioneer and former Harvest Moon Ball finalist.

Grandfather of Vogue William Leake, the legendary Willi Ninja, is widely celebrated for embodying the best of drag ball culture, in the public eye. He also brought club moves to the concert stage, dancing in works by choreographers Karole Armitage, Doug Elkins, and David Neumann. Ninja coached Naomi Campbell and also Paris Hilton with her famous walk. He died at 45 of AIDS-related heart failure. Look-alikes carry on in his memory.

Jennie Livingston's 1990 *Paris Is Burning* featuring Ninja brought the balls above ground. Madonna's song and music video "Vogue" (number one on the Billboard charts in 1990) celebrated and popularized the style. But Malcolm McLaren's 1989 song "Deep In Vogue" predated Madonna's. Ninja's dance in the "Deep In Vogue" music video inspired Madonna among others. The 1989 song appealed to artists, aficionados, costumed club kids, and clubutantes, as well as dance lovers. However, it did not achieve the mass appeal of the commercially backed "Vogue," with its facsimile dance.

AIDS took its toll on the ball community. The Houses put on benefit events. Spike Lee sponsored the Grandest Grand March, a fashion show at the Palladium. The 1989 Love Ball at Copacabana, organized by Susanne Bartsch, raised money for AIDS and found homes for the homeless.

The notion of a Grand March harks back to straight ballroom tradition, court dances, and the ballet *défilé*. The walks feature fluid, angular poses that recall the friezes of ancient Egypt and African dance.

Hustle Dance

In the Bronx, New York, women dancing on neighborhood street corners were creating the Hustle, the partner dance that gave form to the disco era. In 1973, at the Grand Ballroom, women were dancing a new "touch" or partner dance. It was a simple six-count dance with a very basic form and included inside and outside turns. The men were interested in the return to romance and in meeting the women. Latinos went to the Tony Ramone's Corso, Ipanema, Cheetah, and Barney Google's where "Good Taste in Dress [was] Required." Dancers were doing Mambo, Salsa, and Cha-Cha. The new Hustle dance took

Mambo's ball-change and its intricate patterns and turns. It was called the Rope Hustle at first because of the partners' curvilinear arms, flicking hands, and frequent, sharp, quick, changes in direction and hand positions. The six counts evolved as 1-2-3 & 4-5-6. Latino ballet dancers added long balletic arms in the following years.

Disco spread over the nation, and dance contests further refined and defined the style. The clubs hired the original Hustle dancers to entertain and perform, which fueled the craze for the new dance. In 1975, they were invited to dance on TV shows and as guests on talk shows like *Merv Griffin Show*. Then Griffin's *Dance Fever,* and other shows featured them weekly.

In early Hustle dances, the partners stood side by side with the man's arm around the woman's waist and her hand on his shoulder. The partners' relationship, and the dance, became more circular around the mid-1970s. As dancers' skills increased, they added acrobatic tricks and jazz adagios to wow audiences and judges in the ever-proliferating discotheque dance contests.

By splitting the count into & 1-2-3 & 1-2-3, couples had more time to transition into and out of their innovated pyrotechnic moves. They were choreographing, creating a routine of the basic steps and more. They styled with pivots and travelling moves from smooth ballroom and Latin rhythm dances (Fajardo n.d.).

Former Hustle champion Barry Douglas wrote that it is easier for beginners to start with a straight six counts. Hustle "does not move with the beat, but cuts through the beat right to the count, with the movement emphasis of each step being equal, like the count base of the 4/4 music it was designed for," he commented on an FAQ page on Hustle. The best Hustle dancers follow a "built-in pulse." They are slaves to the disco beat that drives the body to conform. Hence, the hiccup or "&," where a preparatory half step back on the ball of the foot, a ball-change, rectifies the dance with the music (Douglas 1999).

Confusion about the count, and teachers' zealous inventiveness, made the dance too complicated for many beginners and for the 1970s notion of group participation. The Hustle became sophisticated, elite, and exclusive as professionals strove to retain its purity within a field of versions and fusions. Those who saw its sudden, mass popularity as a fleeting fad did not put effort into standardizing the method and count, which nevertheless evolved as a simple & 1-2-3.

Although the massive interest in dance was a boon to Hustle dancers, they had mixed feelings about their association with disco. When

disco turned taboo at the end of the 1970s, they were unable to culti-
vate interest among nondancers on the outskirts of the floor. Schools
closed, and dancers insulated themselves in a community that was
fractured but very much alive.

To date, Hustle is considered the last American partner dance to
take hold in our cultural history. It is an anomaly among partner
dances because it refuses to fit the musical phrasing. At this writing,
it is extant, debated, and still a way for people to meet, a vigorous
workout, and an adrenalin boost that generates just as much joy.

Ralph Lew, Harvest Moon Ball, and Hustle

In 1973, the popularity of ballroom dance was such that four Roseland
ballrooms featured Harvest Moon Ball Preliminary contests on four
nights. Rodney Dangerfield, Debbie Reynolds, Natalie Cole, and Tony
Bennett appeared in support of the event. Contestants had to be over
17, wrote Jack Smith who covered the ball for the *Daily News* while
the New York News Charities sponsored it. The proceeds were
donated to charities.

In 1974, dancing was still cheap entertainment. The *Sunday News*
advertised $3.50–$7.50 tickets to the preliminaries at Roseland.
Machito played. Donna Cardi, a nursing student from Ozone Park,
won all-around that year, in the four ballroom categories (Fox Trot,
Tango, Viennese Waltz, and Rumba). A five-member panel judged
contestants, giving up to 20 points for (1) posture and appearance,
(2) rhythm and tempo, (3) execution, and (4) variety. The finals were
at Madison Square Garden, and the jackpot was $6,950. The next
spring, the *News* sent form letters to ticket requesters telling them the
event was discontinued for economic reasons.

Nevertheless, Dick Raymond from the Arthur Murray studio saw a
lot more young people dancing. "Everyone wants to hold on," he said.
Murray had introduced a "disco-touch program" in the studio. He
described it as contact dancing to rock music (Rella 1974).

At the Albert Butler Studios on West Fifty-seventh Street, touch
dancing was second nature for Albert and Josephine Butler. She had
judged the 1936 Harvest Moon Ball. He was among those who thought
the popular 1970s dances could be taught. The Butlers saw nothing
new in the fact that people were dancing together. "While many
people think that the Hustle brought back social dancing, it has never

Ralph and Lucille Lew teaching Latin Hustle at Ipanema, 1975. Photograph by Charlie Gonzalez. (Courtesy of Raíces Latin Music Museum, New York)

really been that far away." Ron Forella was teaching Hustle at Bloomingdales. Lessons were $4. Carol Culver, a cheerleader in *Grease*, was teaching Hustle, Rope, Bus Stop, and others. Jo Jo's Dance Factory was on 721 Broadway. Jo Jo Smith's mother was a Katherine Dunham Dancer, and Jo Jo trained with her since age 13. He charged $5 for a two-hour class during which he played "the latest disco music on his conga drum." The class was full of Broadway chorus line dancers.

At Roseland, Olga Varvaro demonstrated Hustle from a stage on Wednesday and Friday evenings, and Saturday at 2:00. "It's a beginning for young people. A whole generation has grown up knowing nothing of ballroom dancing," she said to *Town & Country*. A night of dancing at Roseland cost $3.50. A Latin band played half-hour sets. The *Town & Country* writer marveled that the new clubs were not as exclusive and that disco dancing was romantic and opulent, "at least in spirit." She visited Roseland with its finest dance floor of maple over 12 inches of cork. "Roselanders are now into the Hustle," she said (Birmingham 1976).

At Ipanema, college students met to Hustle on the polished parquet floor amidst tropical plants. They came for Ralph Lew's Tuesday night dance contest. Tropicalia had live plants, wicker furniture, and a "high caliber membership." The Brazilian owner Peter Martins had Carmen

Cuban-born Ralph Lew is the renowned Latin music producer, dance show producer, and dance instructor. He taught at Catskills, Borsht Belt Resorts and The Pines and Grossinger's, in Tony and Lucille Colon's concession. He worked in their Fifty-seventh Street studio and gave small group lessons on Broadway, doing business as the Ralph Lew Hustle Society. Then he started the Ralph Lew Hustle Factory in Brooklyn. When he and his wife and dance partner Lucille performed with Vince Montana, Jr., and The Salsoul Orchestra at Radio City Hall, the crowd went wild (Vincent Montana 2004). Lew brought along Floyd Chisholm and Nelly Cotto, "the darlings of hustle" (Bess n.d.). *New York* magazine described Lew's 10 p.m. lesson at Ipanema as a mob scene.

D'Allesio organize parties, which she would later do at Studio 54. Birmingham called Tropicalia "fun, breezy, and a teeny bit wicked." The Upper East Side club and other popular Latin clubs had contests and offered free lessons and floor shows in the mid-1970s.

At the Corso, on East Eighty-sixth Street, Birmingham found the "hottest Latin beat in town." Geoffrey Holder went to watch the young stars dancing to Tito Puente. It was "a place to pick up the latest dance steps from Spanish Harlem." Membership at Regine's was pricier at $600. On disco night, dancers could dance from 10:30 p.m. to 4 a.m. for $10 in dressy attire. At Murray the K's Disco on Wheels, Gloria Gaynor demonstrated steps on screen. The important thing was that "On to the scene has come the Hustle, a dance which in spite of its suggestive name, is subtle and smooth. The rhythm is basically six beat with a sweet drive . . . . Dancers move together touching and the steps must be learned. People are discovering that needing people is fun."

The English language *Latin NY* magazine featured Hustle in its December 1975 issue. At the time, said publisher Izzy Sanabria over phone, the Spanish media was ignoring the new dance. Lew, in his *LNY* article on its history, wrote that the Hustle was born when Puerto Rican kids from Spanish Harlem were incorrectly doing their parents' ballroom dances, Cha-Cha, and Mambo. In the early 1970s, teenagers were dancing singly, inventing steps on the floor and improvising.

Young Latinos applied this sense of experimentation to their parent's partner dances and came up with Hustle.

In the issue, writer Aurora Flores championed Hustle. "It has form, grace, posture, and syncopation," as compared to the bouncy freestyle boogaloo and jerk. "The Latin Hustle is a good way to introduce 'Salsa' into the non-Latino world."

Lew was a pivotal figure at the intersection of disco and ballroom. He took up the fight for the Harvest Moon Ball after the competition lost its *News* financial support in 1975 (Haber 1976). The National Council of Dance Teachers stepped in as producer after a hiatus. On Lew's recommendation, they added a Hustle category. Tony and Susan Marolda were the first Hustle winners. The next year, Miguel Marrero and Annette Elias won first place in the Hustle division, against 94 couples from all over the world. Hustle remained in the contest through 1982.

In 1981, as the Ball's executive director, Lew presented a "World of Dancing Hall of Fame" in the Felt Forum as the entertainment for the ball contest, where some of his dancers from Ipanema were competing. Lew coordinated the fiftieth and last Harvest Moon Ball at Madison Square Garden in 1984. "When you go to a disco, you see all these young people and we wish we could get them to come," he said (Caldwell 1984). Ralph and Lucille worked to keep the dance alive. According to a post on the Web site of Nightlife Sounds, they were giving Thursday night lessons at Jimmy's Bronx Café to a mature crowd in 2000.

After winning a contest, a dancer is a pro. Professionals choreographed acts or performed choreographed acts on shows. Because of the popularity of disco music and disco dancing, the audience celebrated Hustle dancers and recognized their artistry. Dancers made a livelihood of Hustle.

Ron Bess was a Harvest Moon Ball Hustle finalist in 1980 and 1981. He had just joined Lew's company and was performing in the Hall of Fame show. Bess danced with the company until 1985. Aside from the ball entertainment, Lew sent couples to perform at weddings, discos, and hotels in New Jersey, Pennsylvania, and the Catskills. Lew "owned the Catskills," said Bess. Bess went from one hotel to another, in a single night, putting on shows. Up to eight couples would provide the entertainment, or open for another act, depending on the client's budget. Each couple performed the same routine. Night Tracks, a New Jersey disco, had regular exhibitions by Bess and Lisa Zimmerman.

Philly Dance

Bess grew up in Philadelphia and watched *American Bandstand* as a boy. He learned to dance in the teen clubs like The Tunnel or another in a converted roller rink around 1974 or 1975. At first, the kids dressed up and did line dances. Dancing with a partner, they would just hold hands and rock back and forth. In 1978 and 1979, he was going to Someplace Else, Gatsby's, or Widow's Watch in the Cherry Hill, New Jersey Area. "There were no teachers back then, you just went in there and danced." By then people were doing the Hustle, and Bess learned at first by copying and then adding his own improvisations (Bess 2010).

Bess went on to dance on *Soap Factory* and Ed Hurst's Atlantic City *Steel Pier Show*. He represented Philadelphia on *Dance Fever* with Zimmerman and was placed in other national competitions. He competed against Eddie Vega and Floyd Chisholm in preliminaries for the Harvest Moon Ball. Bess used his winnings to finance his education. Then, by day, he fitted customers with glasses; at night, he was on the dance floor.

Dancing in Lew's company, Bess learned new tricks and fancy steps to dress up his Hustle routines. He took classes in New York—jazz with Phil Black and Frank Hatchett. He learned adagio at Shelley's New York Hustle.

Bess was dancing competitively from 1979 to 1984. Before exhibitions, he would be on the floor dancing with everybody. Meanwhile, the dancers were "protective and secretive of our routines. We all competed against each other but we're still friends," he marveled. They danced so often, there was little time for grudges. "We all took turns [winning]," said Bess's sometime dance partner Donna Boyle.

As a Philadelphia teen, Donna Boyle (a.k.a. Disco Donna) was also sneaking into the nearby Jersey clubs where they were not strict about carding. "Philadelphia is a big dance town. We had a six-count dance in the sixties with a tap step. We had *Bandstand*," she said (Boyle 2009).

When she came of age, Boyle went to the Philly clubs Shady Lanes, CC Charley's, Library, La Dolce Vita, Second Story, and the upscale Valentino's. "We lived it in Philly." Ron and Lisa, Jose Gonzales and Marcy, Tony and Donna, and Bob and Jeannie were all competing.

On a typical, mid-1970s night in Philadelphia or South Jersey clubs, Boyle participated in a few line dances to soul music and danced the Hustle for the rest of the time. Around 1976, the music started to change.

All the clubs were playing disco, and everyone was doing the Hustle. She and her friends would watch and dissect the dancers' moves.

Then Boyle's set entered contests every week. They performed on the Center City TV show *Discophonic Scene* hosted by radio DJ Jerry Blavat. They made the trip to the Brooklyn, New York, studios Dale and the larger Walter Darian. She continued the weekly trips and danced with David Padilla. They were partners on *Dance Fever* and finalists in the 1982 Harvest Moon Ball Hustle division. *Saturday Night Fever* got them teaching and performing work.

When Hustle started to die out in the 1980s, Boyle and Philadelphia dancers continued to meet weekly. They did not let it die.

New York Constellation

Dancer and native New Yorker Derrick Allen remembered that in the beginning, around 1972 or 1973, "Everywhere you went, [the Rope Hustle] was what people were doing. That was the dance. As kids, we competed, watched each other. After a while, there's a respect that forms, a bond."

In the late 1970s, Allen was encouraged when he competed at Cherry's in Glen Cove, Long Island, and won two Corvettes for himself and his partner and girlfriend at the time, Lilia Parra. He would go to the clubs to meet women; he met Parra there. He had to dance well; he did not want to sit out. Allen started out winning contests at the small clubs that had sprouted up every few blocks in Queens, where he lived. He went to Lemon Tree and Elephas. At the time, there were no computer games and other competing recreational activities. As he saw it, dancing was the only social activity available.

You could go out every night, bouncing from club to club. At the best clubs, for example, Ipanema, Elephas, or Cork & Bottle, "you had to cut it or you would stand on the sidelines." Once the women saw him Hustle, they would ask him for a dance. Cork & Bottle advertised as "New York's most elegant Latin Discotheque." The East Fifty-second Street dancehall featured a Saturday night contest with cash prizes. At Ipanema, the grand prize was $500 at the First Interclub Salsa and Latin Hustle Contest in December 1975. Notoriety came with winning contests. It was not long before Allen was paid $150 per night to dance with the lady club patrons. With that and his prize winnings, he financed his college education.

The studios then invited Allen—Hustle Explosion in Franklin Square and Jeff and Donna Shelley's New York Hustle, Inc. "They would apply a structure to what we were doing," he said. He learned how to communicate with his partners and how to pass the dance on to others. He learned the terminology taught in the studios around 1976.

When *Saturday Night Fever* came out, it stigmatized Hustle. At the same time, it revived the industry by bringing people into the studios. "From a social standpoint, you saw young kids light up a floor with what was truly a new dance" (Allen 2009).

Susan Marolda had studied ballet, jazz, and tap before learning ballroom from Joe Mehegan at age 8. By 14, she was dancing with Tony, who had seen her in a Mehegan competition. Tony and Nick, brothers from Howard Beach, had qualified to move to the finals for the 1974 Roseland Harvest Moon Ball. Tony learned Hustle from Ralph Lew. Susan set a trend with her red sequined Vegas body suit. "Tony's machismo and powerful interpretation" complemented Susan's "striking beauty" and "contagious smile," wrote Ron Bess. "They had the look" (Bess n.d.).

After Hustle was added to the Harvest Moon Ball competitions, Tony and Susan took the All-Around title, winning the four ballroom and the Hustle competitions. They went on to win a contest at Regine's club, after which Regine flew them to France to perform. They competed in Blackpool (England) and took second place in Hustle. After working with Pierre Dulaine, they returned to Blackpool to win in the Theater Arts Division. Tony and Susan appeared on *Soap Factory* and *Soul Alive*, and performed in the pilot episode of the new *Dance Fever*. They opened a studio and ran it together for 10 years. Tony produced "The American Star Ball" competition in 1980. He then moved on to swing and country styles, with a new partner. Susan won a Lifetime Achievement Award at the International Hustle and Salsa Competition in 2007. She has judged national competitions (Bess n.d.).

Eddie Vega's claim to fame is winning $100,000 on *Star Search*, where he danced to "Slave to the Rhythm" with Lisa Nunziella. He held a record, winning 13 times. Vega was a New York street dancer who became a ballroom champion, dancing with Nelly Cotto. The two danced with Ralph Lew's company. He danced in films including *Dirty Dancing*, appeared in *Don Kirshner's Rock Concert*, and won big on *Dance Fever* in 1981. Vega won the Harvest Moon Ball with Lourdes

Jones. He also danced with Maria Torres. Hustle dancer Robin Amante remembers Vega and Jones offering tips when they shared a rehearsal space. Vega contracted AIDS and left this world at age 29 in 1992 (IHDA n.d.).

Ricky Quintana was 15 when he saw Billy Fajardo and Sandra Rivera perform at Radio City Hall; he knew then that he would live to be a Hustle star. He went to Ipanema where he met his partner Lee Rafrano. Ricky and Lee danced a televised *Soul Alive* contest. They went on to represent New York City on *Dance Fever*. The next year, Floyd Chisholm and Nelly Cotto invited the couple to join their dance revue, The Disco Dance Stars. Eddie Vega took him under his wing, and Ricky met a new partner at Odyssey, Lisa Nunziella. The two went on to win ballroom championships. He danced in the movie *Can't Stop the Music*.

Bess called Bronx-born Nelly Cotto "the premiere hustle dancer of our time." South Bronx girls developed the Hustle, which had no turn patterns at first. The girl did all the movement around the male. Cotto learned the Hustle at age 13, from her sister, in 1974. That year, at Butterfly Discotheque, she met Floyd Chisholm. Several years later, the couple competed at Copacabana, with the best dancers from nine clubs, and won. Merv Griffin flew Floyd and Nelly to Hollywood to compete on *Dance Fever*. They danced to the 1978 soundtrack *Thank God It's Friday*, after which the company gave them gold records and named them King and Queen of Disco. They formed the Disco Dance Stars troupe, with founding members Quintana, Nunziella, Danny Llaurado, Carol Famiglio, Eddie Espinosa, and Barbara Procopio. Floyd and Annette Rivera are renown for their dancing in the 1977 movie *Roseland*. Nelly later competed with partners Eddie Vega and Kenny Gonzales, with whom she won $20,000 in a Newport Dance Contest. Nelly performed for Prince Rainier in Monaco with Artie Phillips and with John Leguizamo in the 2002 made-for-TV *Sexaholix*. Bess called her "a living daredevil" and credits her with helping to kill the *Saturday Night Fever* myth. "There is more to hustle dancing then just pointing your finger," says Bess (IHDA n.d.).

Former World Champion William Billy Fajardo was there at Hustle's inception, and he is still on the scene, running competitions in Puerto Rico and in Florida, where he is based, with partner and show dancer Katie Marlow.

Fajardo and Bobby Morales did high rock, a battle dance, in the Parkchester section of the Bronx around 1972 or 1973. The girls on the block showed him dances they had learned on *Soul Train* and a plain, six-count dance they were doing to "Do The Tighten Up." The sheer, normally prohibited, act of grabbing a girl was part of the draw to the adolescent boy. They danced the Hustle to Frankie Vallee's "Swear To God" at red light house parties. Billy liked to listen to Barry White, Lou Rawls, and the orchestral, romantic, songs of the day. He started competing in the small clubs but at age 16, in 1973, he had his first nightclub experience at Grand Ballroom.

Latin groups were playing between sets at Grand Ballroom and at Roseland with an uptempo beat. The fast rhythm aided dancers who, fueled by drugs and alcohol, wanted to show their flair. In 1974 and 1975, Fajardo saw the ball-change and syncopation added to the simple Hustle. He was dancing with Sandra Rivera, and admirers backed him in putting together a performing group called Dance Dimensions, the first televised dance team.

After *Saturday Night Fever*, Fajardo could put on a white suit and make money. He toured Europe for a year and a half with *Saturday Night Fever Live,* but meanwhile, he lamented the way the dance got lost. "They started breaking into line dance, which was never a part of it, and pointing the finger like John Travolta. You don't see Hustle anywhere. Because of that we are the laughing stock of the dance world," said Fajardo at the fifth New York Hustle Congress. "I disengage from anything associated with disco . . . . I didn't wear those shiny clothes and big Afros. We wore suits with pleated pants, chains, expensive flat shoes, and straw hats." He went to Jo Jo's Dance Factory on Broadway between Fifty-fifth and Fifty-sixth streets, Gregory Hines's Hines and Hines, which later became Broadway Dance, Dale Dance Studio in Brooklyn, and Darian Studio. He looked up to Hustle dancers Floyd and Annette (Fajardo 2009).

Trouble with drugs curtailed Fajardo's dancing days, until he met Katie at a Hustle USA weekend in New York. She showed him it was possible to dance without triggering unhealthy drinking and drugging, and he rekindled his love for dance. At the Puerto Rico Hustle and Salsa Festival, he wanted to remerge Hustle with Latin. He wanted to encourage young people with sharp choreography. For Fajardo, the dance goes by the name "Latin Hustle."

Lori Brizzi aimed to unite Salsa and Hustle in the New York Hustle Congress she started in 2004 with the late Salsero David Melendez. Brizzi had danced in Pierre Dulaine's American Ballroom Theater for five years and held Hustle and ballroom champion titles, including prestigious Zachary's awards. She and Sandra Rivera, Billy's partner on *Don Kirshner's Rock Concert*, were inducted into the Hustle Hall of Fame as "champions and hustle divas" in 2009.

Artie Phillips was a beloved member of the Hustle community who passed away in 2008 with AIDS at only 49. His theatrical choreography and his Hustle partnering expressed his generous spirit. In the many YouTube videos, one can see the open chest that is also memorable in Martha Graham dancers Merce Cunningham and Paul Taylor. Phillips' fearless acrobatic acumen enabled a palpable feeling of security in the women he danced with: Nunziella, Elizabeth Darchi, and others. Hustle dancers remember a dance with Artie and name him as a favorite partner. Even after death, he adds his glow. He and Maria Torres danced Hustle together at age 17. Artie danced in the Miss America Pageant, performed and choreographed in Broadway shows, and is a five-time *Star Search* finalist. He was "fierce, fearless, and flawless," said Raymond Del Barrio at his memorial tribute. He was a "patient teacher," said his mother, Elizabeth Halbreich, about the early years when he taught and performed at Arthur Murray and Fred Astaire studios. He then trained with Phil Black and appeared in *Grand Hotel* on Broadway. "The phone was always ringing for Artie."

Back in the day, New York Hustle and Dale Dance Studio advertised Hustle lessons. Henry Dior owned Dale studios on Fifth Avenue, in Elmhurst, Queens, and in Levittown. Classes had around 25 to 45 students with males outnumbering females. Jeff and Jack Shelley opened the first Hustle dance studio in Flushing, Queens, in 1972. "It was the hip hustle studio. All the young people from the clubs were coming in," said Donna Shelley over phone from her Florida home. Club goers were finding that they could not pick up the dance themselves, by just watching. Barry Skeist, a radiologist, was taking lessons because "The dance floor is the last bastion of true male chauvinism acceptable to women" (Alexander 1981).

In the clubs, "we would watch and dissect it. We mixed it up. Instead of dancing learned patterns, we improvised; we played. When you understand the music you can play," said Maria Torres, a first-generation Hustle dancer. She was preparing for her workshop at the 2009 International Hustle and Salsa Competition (Marlow and Fajardo's spring Florida event). In "Hustle the Latin Way," male and female participants faced each other, with Torres in the center, turning to each group to demonstrate. She had rolled one black bell-bottom pants leg up to the knee to show the mechanism and positioning of her sandaled foot. Torres made use of an experienced dancer in the front ranks. Facing the men, she demonstrated an "anchor step" back. She led the women, using her hips to get more freedom of movement. The participants practiced launching into solo circular walks and finally paired off, falling in to the music's beat.

Around 1975 or 1976, the Shelley brothers saw Donna dancing at Murray the K's Hustle club on East Seventy-ninth Street and offered her a job. She was 18 and in college when she started training as an instructor at Shelleys New York Hustle, Inc., studio. Billy and Sandra, George Velasquez, Craig Lee, Floyd, Ron Bess, Derrick and Lisa, and Tony and Susan were there taking or teaching class. The school taught a more polished, technical, exhibition style with lots of lifts and tricks. "We were interested in movie musicals, Fred and Ginger, Gene Kelly. We started putting in the lifts, incorporating the smooth style into hustle." It was classy and elegant. All the couples on the floor had a different style.

Donna worked with François Szony and the tap teacher Henry LeTang on theatrical tricks to put into Hustle. She and Jeff were dance partners and then married. In 1976, they "help[ed] further the Hustle Craze and the public's desire to get involved with the new dances" in a three-record set "Do The Hustle." The instructor's voice and the music are on separate adjustable stereo channels and the third record is just music. More from the liner notes:

[The Hustle Factory] chose America's famous dance troupe, the New York Hustle, Incorporated to create the Hustle dance instructions. This

Jeff and Donna Shelley demonstrate on the 1976 instructional LP *Do The Hustle*. (Donna Shelley)

team of dancers has exhibited the latest steps and taught thousands on television, in Madison Square Garden and in the top clubs and arenas of America. Now they are ready to teach you on this recording. (Discogs n.d.)

The Shelleys demonstrated on the television show *Soap Factory* in 1978 and 1979, where they taped about 80 segments. They opened New York Hustle, Inc., studio franchises in New York and the boroughs. When the Hustle craze died down, they closed them and taught in their Brooklyn home studio. They put together an act and performed on cruise ships in the mid-1980s. In 1989, they met Yvonne Marceau and Pierre Dulaine who had won a part in Tommy Tune's *Grand Hotel*. They needed a couple to replace them in their American Ballroom Theater show. The Shelleys took over their parts and stayed for five or six years in dancing roles created for them by Graziella Daniele and others. There they met Hustle dancers in a core group who are still active teaching and performing today. Donna, at this writing, gives private lessons. She performs with the Rhythm Chicks.

Dance Forever

Floyd and Nelly brought the dance above ground in Merv Griffin's *Dance Fever*. Billy performed "our dance" every week on *Don Kirshner's Rock Concert*, just before *Saturday Night Fever* came out. Eddie Vega and Artie Phillips put Hustle on stage at Radio City Music Hall. Lisa Nunziella won *Star Search*. "Now *we're* the statespeople," said Derrick Allen (Allen 2009).

Thirty years later, Boyle leads a troupe of young competing couples. Salsa dancers are mixing the original Latin style back into Hustle and making it into something new, she said. Boyle had learned from competitors on the floor; they shaped the Hustle. She founded Disco America in 1998. She and Joyce Szili direct the annual Independence Day Weekend King of Prussia, Pennsylvania competition and festival.

Brizzi's New York Hustle Congress shared the New York Hilton weekend with the larger, richer Salsa Congress for its first five years. In 2010, it subsumed the smaller event, which was forced to secede. The New York Hustle Congress moved to a nearby hotel. Brizzi's stalwart event is familial fun and raises money for her charity of the moment.

Bess can still do a split, at this writing. His partner is his teenage daughter, Lauren. He also emcees and judges competitions. "As an emcee, I get to interact with all these dancers," he said. He started the newsletter and syndicated blog, *Dance Talk*, as a way to get the fractured community of Hustle dancers back together and keep the dance alive. He considers the "Hustle Hall of Fame" he created, published by dancer Mark James's Web site, his greatest accomplishment.

"When I was growing up, in New York it was always called Latin Hustle. I don't even know where this description of New York Hustle began . . . for that matter," said Bess in a 2008 *Dance Talk* interview with Allen. Allen answered that the fundamental flavor, understanding, and root of the dance is New York. "We gave it a certain look and feel."

Instructors hope to preserve the integrity of the original. Young dancers who learned from the previous generation of Hustle dancers, of course, want to make it their own. They are to be found in new teen or young working people's clubs, dancing to contemporary music or music selected by DJ peers.

Dancing *Saturday Night Fever*

"Everyone in the 2001 Odyssey disco in Bay Ridge, Brooklyn, seems possessed of a similar short-term vitality and pride. Their dancing is fluid, but it's also strictly, almost militaristically choreographed: people who stake everything on style can't afford to be sloppy, or even genuinely boisterous," said Janet Maslin in her *New York Times* review of *Saturday Night Fever* (Maslin 1977).

Nik Cohn took a guide to research a story he would submit to *New York Magazine*—the story that inspired the movie *Saturday Night Fever*. He recruited an African-American dancer called Tu Sweet. He had seen the "black Nureyev" at a city club performing "loops and dips, double takes, sudden freezes, ebbs and flows." They did not get a welcoming reception when they found Odyssey, a club they had heard about. Cohn felt out of place there and observed for only a few weekends before turning in "Tribal Rites of the New Saturday Night," about the fictional character Vincent, but billed as nonfiction journalism.

Later Cohn told the musicologist Alice Echols that the dynamics in the club were very male dominated and that the girls waited around the dance floor, facing forward in a "military phalanx." His character Vincent sets the formations and dictates the moves on the dance floor, where he is king. They perform what Cohn called the Odyssey Walk. Echols suggests that he based his description, in part, on British Mod dances he knew and the movie *Clockwork Orange* (Echols 2010, 163). Cohn felt alien and regarded the Brooklyn club dancers as alien. His sketchy, fantabulous article looked at disco condescendingly, but *Saturday Night Fever* imparted something loveable and desirable. It made a phenomenon of disco.

"Now shape up you a-holes, we're the faces," says Tony as his group enters Odyssey in the movie. They take over a table. The dancing on the floor is freestyle. Hips rotate and the dancers turn 360 degrees to face each other at intervals. He and Annette partner in a choreographed dance to "Disco Inferno." Tony pumps his pelvis and they dance in unison side by side, freezing in an open position. Tony walks off with his arms raised, as if to tell us, "the women will adore you when you dance."

Two turns into three on the floor, and then all form a line dance. The arm goes up and down diagonally across the torso, with the index finger extended in the up position. It is the Odyssey Walk that Cohn wrote

Karen Gorney and John Travolta in *Saturday Night Fever*. (Photofest)

about. Their line dance is a box walk with their arms flapping like a chicken. Everyone on the floor dances it in unison, all facing the same way.

Later, Tony sits at the bar watching a stripper dance in a niche above while DJ Monti III plays a jazzy instrumental. The stripper does a more fluid Pony, stepping to each side within her small niche. Later, on the floor, two dance topless side by side to "If I Can't Have You," moving alike in this manner, with fluid arms, very frontal, open, cool, and languid.

At the studio, Stephanie and Tony practice Latin, New York, and Tango Hustle to "More Than A Woman." She shows him a Latin dance with a kick. They tango with fancy lifts and dips. Then, looking into each other's eyes, their arms reach out toward each other. They hold hands for dear life. Their plank-like bodies cantilever outward from the center where their feet pivot, and they go round with centrifugal force and speed. Well, disco and Hustle are all about inventing new steps on the fly and expanding the form.

Maria Torres told Alice Echols that as she watched the movie with a group of friends they were perplexed by the dancing and Tony's moves, which were not the like the ones they were doing or seeing in the clubs. But after the movie, newcomers came into the clubs with Tony's freestyle moves. Torres said, they "killed the ambience" (Echols, 177).

The extra dancers in *Saturday Night Fever* were club regulars, which added to the movie's air of authenticity—even if they were following choreographer's instructions. They went uncredited. One particularly notable dancer was filmed while turning; the camera closed up around her knees, showing the swirl of her red polyester skirt. Joseph Pugliese and Adrienne Framet are the Latin couple Hector and Marie. Pugliese, a.k.a. Sergio Jose Chevres, personifies the collision of Italian and Spanish cultures in Bay Ridge. He was teaching jazz dancing at Jo Jo's after the movie opened.

Connie was Fran Drescher's first role. She asks Travolta if he is as good in bed as he is on the dance floor and then dances with him. Drescher went on to a prolific career in television. She is best known for her lead role in *The Nanny* series.

Bert Michaels is Pete, the sleazy dance studio instructor. He leads a class of mature, nondancers. His walk is slumped, jazzy, and contracted, alternating with open, raised arms. He brings them down, laughs, and slumps again. They step side to side, walk forward and back, while opening and then pulling in the arms and chest. Tony later finds Pete dancing debonairly with his girl Stephanie. Michaels was Snowboy in the 1961 *West Side Story.*

At first, Travolta was hesitant about taking the role. Although he had always loved watching dance, he did not know if he had the skill to portray a disco king. When Stigwood had his eye on the story and on Travolta, he prepared the actor by having him work for some months learning the latest disco moves with Deney Terrio, a choreographer who would go on to host the TV show *Dance Fever.* When Badham came on board as director, he brought Lester Wilson in to stage the musical numbers and choreograph. Said Travolta to writer Sam Kashner, "I'm the kind of dancer who needs thought and construction—an idea—before I dance. I need an internal story. Lester would put on some music and he would say, 'move with me, motherfucker—move with me!' " (Kashner 2008, 244). Wilson was a respected choreographer at the time, with an Emmy nomination for his work on a Lola Falana TV special. Lorraine Fields is assistant choreographer, and Jo-Jo Smith, the popular New York instructor and proprietor of Jo-Jo-s Dance Factory, is the dance consultant.

"He's taking over again," say his friends, watching Travolta step on to the floor and twaddle his arms at the club goers ringing the floor, inviting them to dance. He pumps his pelvis and does the line Hustle steps by himself, inserting a chicken walk. He slides his legs open, creeps around the lighted floor on his split legs, then arches up to standing with his arms folded in. He does a startling, airborne Russian split. Gathering himself up into a crouching position, he springs up to standing, repeating this Russian folk-style jump a few times, and then struts off. His solo is a call to dance, to "You Should Be Dancing."

In the Odyssey contest, we are presented with three disco styles: black, white, and Latin. The onlookers are likewise segregated. A black couple is first on. They do a controlled, exuberant Bump to a funky song, "Get Down, Baby." The emcee dismisses them to boos from the largest, vanilla corner.

"Now we have Stephanie Mangano and Tony Manero," says emcee Monti Rock III. Tony and Stephanie dance side by side in an open ballroom position. They step backward and pump curved, outside arms at about eleven and one o'clock. Tony turns to face the opposite direction and still side by side, they extend one arm, protectively, across each other's navel area. They turn in this position. Their slow and sexy dance to "More Than A Woman" forgoes all the fancier steps they did in the studio. They tango. He spins her around and levitates her while their faces lock in a kiss. The surroundings blur. They blend in a whirl of love. He is a grave partner. Everyone is transformed. Tony gently segues into an exit and struts off, very erect and puffed up. She trails him with her hand on his shoulder. This is the love that disco aspired to.

The emcee calls Hector and Marie out in the professional manner, first names with the male leading. In their perfect, theatrical dance, they show that Hustle and Salsa are kin. Marie limbos, and her toe points to 11 o'clock as Hector catches her in a dip. They whirl around singly, emanating energy and buzz across the floor. But the judging is rigged. Tony is the favored, Caucasian club hero, and the crowd is gaga over Tony and Stephanie's love bubble. The camera shows us they have entered a world, on the stage, that is all their own.

Travolta did not like the way a stand-in was walking in the opening scene to the song "Stayin' Alive" and had them reshoot it with *him* doing the walk. His purposeful strut embodies the disco downbeat. He knew how Tony would walk. He had been impressed with the way black kids walked down the halls of his high school, Dwight Morrow, in Englewood, New Jersey. In the early 1970s, the school complement was around 50 percent black students. They were starting to wear dashikis, take African names, and raise their fist in the black power sign. The tension was such that tamper-proof light switches were installed in ladies' rooms after several muggings of white girls. Students learned firsthand about racial unrest. Travolta left Dwight Morrow to attend acting school but took away the cool strut of his male, African-American mates.

Travolta's solo is one of the most famous in the history of dance on film. "He was protecting his character and his dazzling moves" when the shot was close-up and his feet were cut off. He did not want anyone to think that a stunt double did it. Stigwood gave him permission to re-edit (Kashner, 247).

The thirtieth anniversary DVD of *Saturday Night Fever* includes a lesson with Dance Doctor John Cassese and partner Janelle Wax. They begin with a dip and demonstrate twirls and a lift. A "Fever Challenge" game guides you through the line dance steps. The dancer in the swing-arms poses is the choreographer and New York City Ballet dancer Edwaard Liang. You could do worse than try to dance the Hustle that Travolta did.

Albert Goldman rightly points out that the *Saturday Night Fever* partner routines were the most disappointing. They were "right off a TV choreographer's pipe rack" (Goldman 1978, 55). Indeed, Terrio did go on to host the show *Dance Fever*. He produced some instructional videos and wrote *Night Moves*, in which he teaches all the moves in Tony's solo, for example, snake-arms, the rock, the slide, the freak, the dog, the spin to knee-drop, and knee walks. The author features a picture of himself and writes that we can learn the moves from him because he and Travolta look alike. For whatever reason, a student of

Tony's moves can probably learn from this comprehensive book. It explains the partner dances in legible diagrams. Hustle is "a sort of ballroom catch-all with a contagious Latin feeling," he says (Terrio 1979, 48).

Hustle has two beats of music to three steps. It is syncopated: 1, 2, & 3, 4, 5, & 6. A smooth leader lets the lady know where to go, says Terrio. The arms should be toned, with the fingers relaxed but moveable. He presents the sugar push, a nudge into a half turn right or left, ending in the open position (side by side), with one arm across the partner's chest. He presents underarm turns, inside and outside, cuddle turns, and a matador turn (he turns her as if she is a cape, her arm is behind her back and she is facing away from him), twist turns with the arms twisted overhead, and crossover turn with the hands held crossed in the center. Then Terrio presents spins done with the above turning patterns. He presents the lateral and death drop, the carry lift, and the shoulder lift.

Terrio had been with the dance troupe The Lockers and worked with Travolta for three hours a night for five months in the studio before the filming, according to *Night Moves*. Terrio gave Travolta the finger-pointing gesture. People somehow connected it to the Hustle, to the dismay of many committed Hustle dancers.

Lester Wilson, who came on the scene later to choreograph the musical numbers, also came out with a book in 1978. In his *Dance Dance Dance* he writes, "Get the routine down pat." His basic Hustle includes a synco step between two beats. All Hustle variations are performed to a six-count rhythm, he says. For this reason, some are surprised to find they can dance the Hustle to waltz music. Latin Hustle has more steps in place, says Wilson. He names an eight-count partner dance, Tango Hustle. He also diagrams Lindy Hustle, Disco Swing, and Disco Duck, a 32-count line dance. The Bus Stop is an 18-count line dance, (partners stand side by side). In The Walk, a 38-count line dance, dancers take a few steps to each side, then rise up on their toes, click their lifted heels, and pivot, repeating three more times in a box pattern.

Roller Disco

New York roller disco originated in the 1970s, when a DJ replaced the organ at Empire, a rink in Brooklyn's Crown Heights neighborhood.

The rink opened in a converted Ebbets Field garage in 1941 and operated until 2007. Its capacity was 2,500. Choreographer Marcellus Williams skated there. People called him the Poet Laureate of Empire. Cher, Ben Vereen, and others came to skate on the crowded floor with virtuosos. Skaters known as Miss Mean Wheels, Pat the Cat, Virgo Black, Ultra Freak, and Puerto Rican Mike were among them (Bleyer 2007).

Marion Green was in his late twenties when Bronx personality Randy Higginson organized bus trips to the Empire Rink. Green was one who became passionate about skating. Early on, Walter Johnson, a classically trained figure skater, taught Green to spin and skate on the edges of his wheels. Another expert, known as C.J., helped him with his footwork.

Green, Julio Estien, and Pam Mitchell saw a team from Baltimore perform. They decided to form their own skate club called the Village Wizards. Michael Bellgrave, Virginia Bovian, Tony Jackson, Sheila Reid (now Reid-Pender), and Melody Waltrous joined, completing the founding troupe.

Richard "Dick" Clammer founded the first wood floor Manhattan rink for neighborhood kids, including his own. Village Skating opened in late summer 1976. It was a basement space at 15 Waverly Place. At first, it was furnished with a couch, an easy chair, and a jukebox. Poles in the center of the long narrow space created a natural, circular traffic flow. The décor consisted of a few disco balls hung among the exposed drainpipes and a wide, red supergraphic on the wall. Skaters relaxed in a small conversation pit. At $4 for admission and $2 to rent skates, it was inexpensive and a good place to learn.

While Empire had a cult following, it was off the beaten path. Village Skating popularized roller disco. Villagers had seen Rollerena skating around in a fairy godmother costume. Adults caught the bug. "It's a rush for some people," said Estien. Virtuoso Empire skaters Pat the Cat, Bill Butler, Slomo, and Vinzerrelli brought their wheels there. Pat the Cat dressed as a cowboy. Vinzerrelli played the saxophone while skating. They were generous about sharing their skills with beginners. Grace Jones, other celebrities, and paparazzi followed. Capacity was about 300 and consisted of all races, ages, and economic classes. "The depth of your skating skills and how much of yourself you were willing to invest to improve those skills," is all that mattered, wrote Green on Estien's Web site (Green, Village Skating n.d.).

A Kentucky teenager known as the Bluegrass Belle skated in clamp-ons. After serving in Vietnam, he settled in New York and found work in the financial district. By the Spring of 1970, at age 22, he had a new, Rockefeller Center Area job, and he travelled to and from it on eight wheels. He was one of the first to skate past rush hour traffic in a suit and tie. In his off-time, the tall, slim New Yorker skated on the piers or in Central Park. His warm weather gear consisted of an umbrella hat, goggles, t-shirt, shorts, and army surplus backpack. "I practiced very hard to dance and skate like that. This is not something where you just put on the skates and . . . you have to be consistent to be good at it," he said (Rollerena 2010).

People called him Rollin' Skeets by the time he took part in the 1971 Gay Pride March. That year on July 4, he first skated in the Village for a change and liked it. In a vintage clothing store in the fall of 1973, he came across an ecru gown that recalled Ginger Rogers. He wore it with a straw hat and carried a basket, drawing stares as he skated down West Village streets.

His costume was complete by the 1973 Easter Parade, when he officially debuted as Roller Arena Fairy Godmother, with 1950s glasses, hat, and the gown. He carried a circus baton wand. On the open piers, he held the wand up, posing like a Liberty figure against the Hudson River. The character's name was simplified as Rollerena.

Rollerena dance skated at the discos and took on a publicist as invitations to New Year's Eve galas and club openings amassed. After a friend at the Studio 54 door invited him to the club's first Halloween Party in 1977, virtually every weekend Rollerena was the moving fixture. His appearance skating in the gown was cause célèbre, and later he was just as welcome dressed "as a regular person." He drank Diet Coke and accessorized from his collection of rhinestone glasses and hats. "You got to keep changing to be interesting," he said. Rollerena attended the opening night at Xenon, Funhouse, Roxy, Palladium, the Saint, and many more.

In 1983, Rollerena started lending his talent to benefit AIDS causes. He had helped New Yorkers transcend troubled times as a pioneer of adult street skating and roller disco and won the first (1988) Saint Lifetime of Achievement, Heritage of Pride Award. In the twenty-first century, he likes the title Queen of Studio 54. He helps organize and attends Center parties and Pride Marches (Gay Center n.d.).

Khalil Kain skated at Village at age 14. "In six months he was better than anyone else on the floor," said Green. "He was strong, smooth, and relaxed. Everything was there for a purpose" (Green 2010).

Kain's Chinese grandfather was a kung-fu stylist, and he himself attained black belt. When he moved on to Roxy and High Roller, he was one of the best. He was then hired to skate dressed as a panda in a TV commercial. He later gained fame as Darnell in the TV show *Girlfriends*. His wide range of roles includes a skating Sister Boom Boom in *The Execution of Justice*, Rahim in *Juice*, a porn star in *The Velocity of Gary*, and twenty-one year old Tiger Woods in *The Tiger Woods Story*.

Green answered a *Village Voice* ad and got the job managing Village Skating. He now had a place to skate for free every day and a salary. By 1977, Estien was mixing records seven nights a week as the club's first DJ and possibly the first DJ using two turntables and playing for skaters.

Otis Salid came into the club, saw the Wizards practicing their routines, and offered to help with dance instruction and choreography. (Salid later gained fame with his "Beat It" choreography for Michael Jackson.) The group went on to perform a "Magic at Metropolis" show, with Western and wedding skits, at the larger clubs. Reid famously skated at Xenon in Gloria Gaynor's 1979 music video "I Will Survive" (Gaynor 1979). Mitchell was a shy girl and never would have gone to Xenon, Studio, Tavern on the Green, or Broadway. She traveled with the Wizards to other cities, Ireland, and Germany. Green and Mitchell helped Reid get started. Then, she and Estien won a contest in Central Park. Macy's saw her and asked her to skate for a Betsey Johnson event. That was her beginning.

Many remember the Wizards, but there were other skating clubs. Kain started the Stylist skating group. Dwight Toppin's group was called the Striders. Fred Tantao and his cousin Nelson were tired of the polyester on disco dance floors and thrilled at the possibilities of dancing on wheels. Tantao came to Village Skating and met Kain, who inspired the style of his group Scramblin Feet, with Larry Pender and Tor Jones, and then Bob Grant. They opened for the Wizards. Reid-Pender was part of Scramblin Feet and the Wizards.

Butler led Goodskates. The group entertained at discos, for example, at Xenon in 1978 and at Bond, where a lesson was included at a 1980 Rollerballroom party. Higginson, known as Dr. Skatemore, was emcee.

There were not many women's groups then, but women were encouraged. Village Skating started a ladies night in 1980. Admission for women was $2, and skate rental was half price. They had all-night skating parties with snacks, juice, and Perrier, and performances by the Wizards and the Feet. The Wizards School of Rollerdancin' was in Jo Jo's Dance Factory, at 1733 Broadway and Fifty-fifth Street. For $90, the six-week course met Saturday afternoons and promised basic dance technique, an exercise component, kicks, jumps, spins, and stops.

Estien played an eclectic blend for the skate clubs. Ballads were popular for romantic pairs. Their dances were fluid and sensual. The music was melodic and the disco songs were long. The skaters on drugs had the patience. Estien played "Good Times" by Chic, "Lover's Holiday" by Change, and Michael Jackson's "Rock With You." His selections ranged from Sinatra to the Doobie Brothers, "What A Fool Believes" and "I Wanna Be Your Lover" by Prince, in his danceable phase.

Estien started working at the larger clubs and spun at the Roxy opening in December 1979. Green followed him there in 1981. The skaters had moved on to the bigger rinks, and Village Skating closed in 1984. Rock promoters backed Roxy, so the music followed suit. The West Chelsea club had been called "the Studio 54 of skating" in its heyday in the early 1980s. The skaters and management were out to create living theater. The door policy was politely selective. No jeans. Roxy served alcohol. It was a place to "skate and feel extremely chic at the same time." Celebrities, laborers, and office workers skated side by side, disco style. On a typical midweek night, 2,000 skated. Flip Wilson, Cheryl Tiegs, or Mick Jagger skated in one of its three rinks. The rinks were connected by ramps. Roxy had theme parties like Las Vegas and a circus night with a live elephant (A. Jacobs 2005).

Diana Ross and Cher skated at Metropolis, where after 11 p.m., advanced skaters were in the rink. At High Rollers, some wore sweatshirts and jeans, and some wore leotards and sequins. As prices rose for a night of roller disco in the more upscale Roxy, Metropolis, and High Roller, Central Park was an option. Renting skates in the Park cost $2.50 an hour, and the skating was free (Johnston 1980).

Roxy became a popular gay nightspot after it closed and reopened again. Skating persisted on Wednesdays. The *New York Times* observed in 2005, "Although acrobatic jam skating is on the rise, the Roxy crowd prefers the old-school dance style, powered by disco and rhythm and blues, with its graceful glides, spins and jelly-limbed leg work" (A. Jacobs 2005). The skating had diminished to one rink, with dancing instead on Saturday night. It closed again in 2007, but that is not to say it is gone for good.

5

Those '70s Shows

Everyone knows that today's artists turn for pleasure not to art but to kitsch.

—Harold Rosenberg, "Pop Culture: Kitsch Criticism"

The popular TV sitcom *That '70s Show* is proof of a retro fondness for the disco era, but there are many tributes and remembrances. Books, art, music, dance, theater, and films sought to materialize, redux, or make sense of the times either observed or memorialized. In the 1970s, boundaries of all kinds were tested, including the one between fact and fiction. Document often seemed inadequate or impossible. *Saturday Night Fever, Roseland, Fame,* and *Summer of Sam* theatricalize reality in a new kind of blend. The fiction, in turn, was telling truth. TV reality dance shows perpetuated the feel-good fantasy conjured by dancing. They had heart and fun, in keeping with the innocence of dancing in the disco era.

Saturday Night Fever

The Son of Sam killer was caught in August 1977, and many young would-be disco dancers breathed a sigh of relief. It was safe to go out at night again. Then, the December release of *Saturday Night Fever* added a rush of health to disco and dancing. Producer Robert Stigwood never imagined his shoestring effort would be a blockbuster.

John Travolta had been contracted to star in three movies: *Saturday Night Fever, Stayin' Alive*, and *Grease*. The makers planned *Saturday Night Fever* as an appetizer, but Travolta created a character of epoch-making proportions in Tony Manero. Janet Maslin called him "a source of fierce, desperate, excitement." She said the movie "has a violent energy . . . best demonstrated in the dancing sequences" (Maslin 1977).

Despite the fact that the film's success was a surprise, director John Badham took the project most seriously, as did Travolta, and the Bee Gees wrote and performed five of the songs. When the Bee Gees finished their work, and Stigwood saw the market potential of the music, he released the double-album soundtrack several months before the opening of the film. The music buoyed the cast's morale. The soundtrack was number one for 25 weeks, outselling any previous record album.

The Australian-born Stigwood was a British music tycoon and had mingled with the disco set. He had made the rock musical films *Jesus Christ Superstar* and *Tommy*. John Avildsen, who was directing at the start, insisted on having Norman Wexler write the screenplay instead of Cohn. British-born Badham took over as director when Avildsen continued to have problems with the cast and crew.

Filming began on March 14, 1977. With the newly invented Steadicam, which Avildsen had used for *Rocky*, the crew could get into tight places, like the corridors of paint cans in the store where Tony worked and his tiny bedroom. Tony has the iconic poster of voluptuous Farah Fawcett on his wall. His father takes a sidelong glance at it, as if to assure everyone of his heterosexuality, in general. It may have also comforted the studio executives, who had balked at the homoeroticism in the bedroom scene in which Travolta wears only black briefs and poses in front of the mirror in the cozy room (Kashner 2008, 254).

Young, Italian-American store clerk Tony comes of age through dancing. He is restless and knows there is more to life than his job. He is king of the dance floor at night. He goes out with his friends in a beaten-up Impala to a Bay Ridge neighborhood disco, where they strut their stuff. Tony leads the patrons in dances and wins a competition. He realizes that another Latino competitor couple were better, and he gives up the trophy and prize money, although they had happily walked away with second prize.

West Side Story comes to mind when Travolta and his friends break into the Barracuda's Lounge to avenge an attack on one of their own.

Everyone comes out with band-aids. It turns out the Barracuda's may not have been the right target. The band-aids scar the boys' faces for the big dance contest. Disco was supposed to be all inclusive, but *Saturday Night Fever* sheds light on the actual segregation in and outside of the clubs.

Annette (Donna Pescow) is so in love with Tony that she suffers tremendously avenging his rejection. He wants to get serious about his dancing and chooses Stephanie (Karen Lynn Gorney) instead as his partner for the contest. Stephanie is a "different" girl whose dancing he had admired at the club. She is the catalyst for the growing up he will do. She moves to Manhattan for a better life and pays the price in more ways than one. Does she really escape mediocrity? *Saturday Night Fever* leaves the question unanswered. Tony wants to follow her, but his crass behavior puts her off. In the tender ending, they are friends. The Verrazano-Narrows and Brooklyn bridges between Manhattan and Queens are metaphors for the hopes and dreams of these Brooklyn native characters.

The perception at the time was that Travolta was just playing himself. The public had underestimated his acting ability. Travolta was so well loved as Vinnie Barbarino in *Welcome Back, Kotter* that crowds of young girls would assemble outside the filming and call "Barbarino!" They had to start shooting at dawn to evade them (Kashner, 246).

At the time, Travolta was dating Diana Hyland, best known as Susan, the alcoholic wife in the soap opera *Peyton Place*. She played Travolta's mother in the made-for-TV movie *The Boy in the Plastic Bubble*. He did not know that Hyland was dying of breast cancer but stayed with her when he found out. She died in his arms, at age 41, on March 27, 1977. She had urged him to take the part of Tony.

Gorney was Tara in an episode of *All My Children*. She had suffered a motorcycle accident injury a few years before the filming of *Saturday Night Fever*, which made the dancing especially challenging. This Brooklyn native, who had actually crossed over into "the city" and relative glamor, lent her share of authenticity to the film.

The film established disco stereotypes like Travolta's white three-piece suit (now in the Smithsonian Collection), his precision blow-dried hair, and his dance-floor moves. The costumer Patrizia von Brandenstein may have seen the suit on Robert Redford in the 1974 movie *The Great Gatsby*, or in *Soul Train*, or in *Roseland*. Deney Terrio stylized the dance moves, and then Lester Wilson helped Travolta put the magnetism in his dancing.

For most of David Berkowitz's murderous year, police had called
the killer at large "the 44 Caliber Killer." He was calling himself
the "Son of Sam" when on July 31, 1977, he attacked two who were
parked near the Verrazano Bridge that features in *Saturday Night
Fever*. The victims had been dancing at the small Bay Ridge club
Jasmine's, not far from Odyssey.

Berkowitz had struck a couple parked near Elephas in Queens
on June 27, 1977. By then, he had killed five and wounded six.
Many New Yorkers responded to, and added to, the hysteria by
becoming amateur detectives during that year. A cult had formed
around it. The concerned met at a dismal bagel shop in Manhattan
plastered with "WANTED" posters. Two of eight attacks were on
disco dancers. The *New York Times* reported that Elephas neighbors ignored the "pop" thinking it had come from the disco. Some
residents of quiet streets with discos already felt animosity toward
them. Yet the door was open when wounded dancer Sal Lupo ran
to Elephas for help (M. Carroll 1977).

After the July 31 attack in South Brooklyn, a neighborhood
woman alerted police to Berkowitz's illegally parked car. Police
finally arrested him on August 11, ending his terrifying, year-long
rampage. Unlike many fearful, outer borough young women,
Gorney was unfazed by Sam. She wrote in an e-mail, "During filming
all I thought about was not getting too cold and pulling a tendon!"

The club women are "assertive," to use a 1970s, women's lib catchword. They approach Tony and ask him to dance, praising his looks
and dancing. Tony and his male and female friends enjoy watching a
stripper dancing on a raised platform above the bar area. It was a
man's world. If women were emboldened, then men were fiercely
guarding their place in the order.

The decade was one of changing values, and *Saturday Night Fever*
successfully mirrored the times, winning its way into people's hearts.
The Latino couple, the best on the floor, should have won the contest.
Saturday Night Fever has Tony recognize the racist fix and right the situation. The movie seeks to break out of homophobic, racist, misogynist
mores, in Tony's dreams of escape across the bridge. It is a mash-up of
old and new ways. All this newfound freedom. What to do with it?

Badham tried different endings and settled on irresolution. The main couple sits in Stephanie's apartment, peering out the window at the city street, and vaguely imagines a better life.

The film discofied America. In 1978, 40 percent of Billboard's Hot 100 was disco. Kids carried disco lunch boxes and slept under disco bedsheets. Musicians of every ilk caught the fever. Frank Sinatra and Ethel Merman made disco records. About 200 radio stations boasted all-disco music, and about 15,000 new discotheques opened. Thousands bought three-piece suits off the rack, coiffed their hair, and learned partner dances.

The critics gave mixed reviews. Maslin sensed a formulaic quality to the Bee Gees music but admitted that at best, it "moves with a real spring in its step, and the movie does too." Aletti thought the songs might renew people's faith in disco. But this would take time. Variety called the movie vulgar and exploitation. Gene Siskel loved it. Critic Andrew Kopkind wrote that the Bee Gees music had "made disco safe for white, straight, male, young, and middle-class America" (Kopkind 1995).

Roseland

Saturday Night Fever spread disco like wildfire. The country was not ready for *Roseland* when it was released on October 2, 1977. Vincent Canby found it "funny," but it did not do well at the box office. It does remain the most authentic and stunning portrayal of 1970s Hustle dancing on film. Almost all of it was shot inside New York's Roseland Ballroom. The camera briefly pans a display with the deco-style letters spelling "Roseland Dance City Wall of Fame" above a row of framed photos and shoes of the great Roseland dancers. Christopher Walken stars as the elegant lady's man.

The film immortalized the young Hustle couple Floyd Chisholm and Annette Rivera. Chisholm is one of several young blacks in the Hustle division, representing their race among the club patrons. He is dressed in a three-piece white suit, a blue ruffled shirt, and a bow tie. Rivera has a swirly light blue dress and white, strappy heels.

Roseland has three parts, Waltz, Hustle, and Peabody. Hustle dancers Chisholm and Rivera play the young couple competing in the Harvest Moon Ball semi finals. They do not win, although they are clearly the best among the (uncredited) amateur contestants. The camera focuses

on Rivera's feet twisting side to side in quick pivots. Chisholm turns
her overhead. She ends with a split on the floor. They are sheer
elegance. Their trainer, Cleo (Helen Gallagher), says they don't look
like they are putting their all into it and advises the kids to come back
the next day to start practice for next year's competition. They do not
protest. Writer Ruth Prawer Jhabvala, director James Ivory, and
producer Ismail Merchant keenly observed the mix of races in the
dance and in the era.

Roseland portrays Hustle as the sparkling new dance of the era that
the young are doing. Meanwhile, the others are reliving their youth
or dancing themselves to death. Emcee Don De Natale is the perfect
gentleman, to the point of morbidity. He and the brass band facilitate
the fantasies, stone-faced. He steps in at the eleventh hour and sweeps
the ladies off their feet. One dies in his arms. He calls for the band to
play on and for everybody to dance.

Chisholm and Annette, too, look perfectly stoic, and possibly dislo-
cated, dancing downtown, having taken their skill to another, per-
formative level. The movie begins with a dance lesson. "They're all
good dancers," says Cleo in an aside. Her lesson is likely modeled on
the ones Olga Varvaro of Pedro and Olga Dance Studio gave several
times a week at the club. Their names appear in the credits. Patricia
Birch is the choreographer and the young Hustle couple dance to the
1974 Cheryl Lynn recording "Super Cool" by Elton John. The rest of
the music is a live, on-the-set, anonymous big band. Vincent Canby
said it is "so romantic that Mr. Ivory makes us accept, in the conclud-
ing episode, an explosion of outrageously overblown sentiment"
(Canby 1977).

Summer of Sam

This excellent, 1999 Spike Lee movie failed at the box office, like
Roseland. It is a love letter to the 1970s and a brash, vivid bricolage in
the Lee manner. Critics have named it one of the top underrated films.
It points at the racism, homophobia, and sexual promiscuity of the era,
through the eyes of Italian-Americans in a mixed, working-class,
outer-borough neighborhood. The main storyline is the hunt for the
mad serial killer Son of Sam who had New Yorkers living in fear from
the summer of 1976 through the summer of 1977. It shows a time in flux,
reflected by an eclectic musical score that includes original compositions

played by a full orchestra, popular disco recordings, and live punk performances.

Hairdresser and sex addict Vinny (John Leguizamo) and his wife Dionna (Mira Sorvino) dance the Hustle. Vinny wears a white suit to the disco. He is the strong character in his group of friends and the only one featured dancing. In the first dance, he leads a confident Hustle. Then, moving out to the edge of the dance floor, they grind and bump against a wall, while Dionna works to please him. Vinny is already heading for trouble with pills and cocaine. The movie suggests this is adding to his increasingly bad sexual behavior.

The young couple goes out for a night to repair their marriage. They are disappointed when a punk band including their friend Richie in a Mohawk (Adrien Brody) is playing. They move on to a special night at Studio, but the line is so long they do not get in, so they end up at Plato's Retreat.

The movie highlights dancers' disappointment when discos did not seem to be about dancing anymore. Instead, the choices were jumping up and down to rock and punk music, rubbing shoulders with celebrities at Studio, or stand-alone sex at Plato's.

The stellar *Summer of Sam* cast includes Bebe Neuwirth, Patti LuPone, Ben Gazzara, Lee, and Michael Imperioli (from *The Sopranos*). Hustle dancers admire Leguizamo's work. The dance instructor is Paul Pellicoro, owner of the respected New York City dance studio Dancesport.

TV Dance

The television shows *American Bandstand, Soul Train, Dance Fever,* and *Soap Factory* were national syndicates. Many kids watched entranced on Saturday mornings, after school, or in the early evenings. It gave them a feeling for dance and the knowhow to approach it.

Soul Train was the brainchild of Don Cornelius, a former Chicago police officer—turned broadcaster. The first show was aired in that city in 1970. Cornelius proposed the name after he had been touring a show to school auditoriums all in one day to save expenses. He had looked at Dick Clark's long-running *American Bandstand* for inspiration, but he did not want to imitate it. He wanted *Soul Train* to be something else, he said in an interview on the new *Best of Soul Train* DVD package. "The blackness of it all is what made it different."

It caught on and Cornelius had the opportunity to move the show to Los Angeles. That city had the technical expertise to upgrade the show for syndication. Not only that, but the talent pool was larger. Everyone wanted to go to Los Angeles and "the dancers from LA, they were wild," said Cornelius. Chicago dancers had to be cool and smooth (Cornelius 2010).

Soul Train was considerably important to disco dancing. Not only were 1970s kids (and their parents) watching on Saturday mornings and acquiring a feeling for dance, but also as Cornelius said, "Watching the Soul Train Dancers was like finding a bird nest on the ground." All America gained access to black culture, previously found only in the living rooms of black families or in black teen clubs that whites did not know about. The awesome dancing ignited teens across the nation. Thus, the show contributed to a more uniform style in discos, where many thousands of dancers owned moves seen on the show (Cornelius 2010).

Jody Watley and Jeffrey Daniel were Soul Train Dancers (they would later join Shalamar). Watley realized her dream to dance on *Soul Train* with much perseverance. She idolized the Soul Train Dancers, and when she spotted Tyrone Proctor on an L.A. street, she asked how she could get on the show. After visiting the set, for some months (they taped one weekend per month), she finally got her chance when Kirt Washington needed a partner. Once she was a regular, she could design her own costumes and moves, which she described as "outrageous." The dancers would pick out costumes from earlier eras in vintage clothing stores. They had formed a team called the Waack Dancers. They practiced on the basketball court and in Mavericks Flat, a popular L.A. disco.

Watley was 16 when *Ebony* magazine featured her, Daniel, Proctor, Sharon Hill, Cleveland Moses Jr., and Washington as the most popular *Soul Train* dancers. For the shoot, the men wore pleated pants or the new Levi's peg legs (501s). Watley wore saddle shoes and socks with a below-the-knee dress. She holds a fan over fellow Waacker June Finch while Ricky Porchia and Cynthia Dright do the Spank. "Their dance moves have been copied everywhere and so have their trendy clothes and unusual hairstyles." A dancer in *Thank God It's Friday* admitted copying Proctor's robotic moves and his kicks and lunges. The *Ebony* writer saw Proctor's moves in John Travolta's *Saturday Night Fever* routines. At the Soul Train Dance Studio in Hollywood, Watley and other Soul Train Dancers taught their moves to the likes of Donna Summer and Cicely Tyson (The "Outrageous" Waack 1978).

Daniel is credited with foreshadowing Michael Jackson's moonwalk. The Jackson Five had performed on the show in 1972 but without the moves that Michael Jackson later made popular. Most likely, he and the Soul Train Dancers influenced each other over the show's 35-year life. The Lockers also traded influence with the Soul Train Dancers who performed their brand of acrobatic break dancing on the show. The Lockers started in 1973 and always prided themselves as street dancers. They assembled a vintage gangster look with striped socks and loose-legged, rolled-up pants to show off the socks. They could fit kneepads underneath. They flirted with clownishness but rejected the clown or minstrel identity.

Dancing is specific to each song and often spontaneous. Improvised line dances form on the spot. To "Kung Fu Fighting" in a 1974 episode, couples throw air punches into the space between them. Dancers raise and lower two arms, in front, to the B.T. Express song "Do It ('Til You're Satisfied)"; the innovative move then sweeps across the dance floor in a flash. A dancer's hand circles above in a kind of lasso move. Gay dancers popularized this move, adding fans. A lanky black male teen in a 1973 episode wears a white suit and a bow tie. He looks like the Hustle legend Floyd Chisholm, and he is one of the few dancing in ballroom position with his partner.

The *Soul Train* dance floor was below the level of a runway-like stage where musical groups performed. At the end of the show, the dancers walk forward on the stage, in twos. The *Soul Train* line was couples' chance to perform a practiced or choreographed act of their dancing—their 15 seconds of fame. It is a runway walk with an acrobatic move, or any variation including voguing, pelvic rotations, robotics, or varied freestyle fancy. *Soul Train* styles had a future.

Although in 1993 Cornelius stepped down as host, the show ran until 2005. He invited Bowie, Elton John, and a few white dancers. The dances and costumes got sexier and sharper. Their tricks got more daring and imaginative. The set was refreshed and high-tech as it segued into the *So You Think You Can Dance* age, where competition was the new theatrical.

The talent pool diffused as dancers found places on MTV and BET. But the show had opened doors for black performers. It outlived *American Bandstand (AB)* and nearly matched its longevity. While that show had been an oasis for American dancing teens in the 1950s and 1960s, in the 1970s the *AB* age limit increased; and it developed a reputation as "a nostalgic memory of dancing times gone by" (Giordano 2007, 224).

Other, short-lived TV dance shows cropped up to help buoy the 1970s new wave of dancing. The following were airing in U.S. cities and noted in Bruce Pollack's 1979 *Disco Handbook*:

Dance Fever—Hollywood

What's New—St. Paul

Soap Factory—New York

Disco Magic—Miami

Hot City Disco—Los Angeles

Soul Alive—New York

The Scene—Detroit

Weekday Fever—Cleveland

Disco 23—Albuquerque

Studio 78—DC

Invitation to Dance—New York

On the East Coast, *Soap Factory* was taped in the Palisades Park, New Jersey, disco, a transformed soap factory. The club décor was a readymade set for the TV show, which ran two seasons from 1977 to 1979. Dancer Zania, commenting on the Web site disco-disco.com, remembers being asked to join the cast. They shot four episodes of the weekly show on one Monday night a month, to create the first season. The young dancer was not paid. She liked to dance and got recognition and experience. A technician also commented that he had done it for love (discomusic.com n.d.).

Soap Factory guest artists, including dance skaters, broke up scenes of good, amateur dancing on the floor. A clip of a show segment, in Donna Shelley's collection, shows the professional New York Hustle Dance Troupe featuring six, Jeff and Donna, John and Linda, Johnny and Donna, in a Hustle routine to "Tailgate" at the club. In their weekly segment, the Shelleys gave instruction or performed, Fred and Ginger style.

In one Shelley segment, Donna does a manège, a chain of turns in the performing ring. Jeff watches as she comes toward him. Resting

Donna and Jeff Shelley on the set of *Soap Factory*. (Donna Shelley)

his foot momentarily on the edge of a first bleacher, he supports her as she flies over his extended leg. Repeating this motif, they continue counterclockwise. Their routine is full of buoyant lifts and turns amidst soap bubbles, blinking, colored lights, and fog effects.

In 1979, for the show's fiftieth episode, the crew and performers went to the nearby Six Flags Great Adventure amusement park to tape a "Dream World" segment. Deniece Williams, Ronnie Dyson, Sarah Dash, and Wardell Piper danced or skated in front of the park's fountains and "Yum-Yum" Palace. Paul Harris was the host (Billboard 1979).

Merv Griffin produced *Dance Fever*. The half-hour show was on at 6:30 p.m. on the East Coast starting in 1979. Deney Terrio was host until 1985. Janet Jones and Diane Day were his costumed partners and incidental, unison dance assistants. Cindy Skogen was one guest DJ.

Contestants from various cities—for example, Jackson, St. Louis, New York, and Minneapolis on one 1982 show—competed in the half-hour slot with choreographed routines. Three celebrities judged, including choreographer Donna McKechnie on show number 26. The judges were nice, and the spirit was noncompetitive.

The décor was balloons, as in the low-tech décor of some discos. The stage was more of a runway than a concert stage, with very little room for traveling moves (in 1982 and 1983). Male–female couples performed the routines. The contestants ranged in age from 18 to 65 and had won auditions held in their cities.

In a 1982 episode, Lisa Nunziella was completely limber and trusting as Daniel Llaurado whipped her around his head and around his feet. He lifted her overhead in a split. Their routine was a string of tricks and near perfectly executed. A Pittsburgh couple brought a line hip-hop routine. From St. Louis, viewers saw a robotic, moonwalking, disco line dance with a ribbon prop and a jazzy dance from Jackson, Mississippi. This last couple's unison dance was more silly than technical. They wore red sequins, and he spanked her.

Cyd Charisse was one of the judges in a 1983 show with Terrio still the star host. Terrio had molded hair and wore a black tuxedo, a bow tie, and a rose in his lapel. This show (year six, number twenty-six) featured dancers from Buffalo, Chicago, and Florida. The Floridian, black couple wore white face. They vogued and mimed to a scratching record in their pop-soul routine. The Chicago dancers wore one blue sequined glove, and their moves nodded to Michael Jackson (a few months after Motown 25 was aired). A Los Angeles couple danced a jazz adagio routine with shades of Hustle. Diane Day graduated to DJ in this show.

Judges gave the finalists scores of 70–100 on originality, execution, and showmanship. The Grand Prize was $25,000. Other winners took home a car, pick-up truck, and stereo system. In 1985, Griffin hired Adrian Zmed to take over hosting. Griffin told a reporter that Terrio was "irrational and undependable." Allegedly, he threatened the company president with a lead pipe, he missed work, and he did not dance with his assistants as much as Griffin wanted. Then in 1991, Terrio tried to sue Griffin for sexual attacks starting in 1978. The judge threw the case out of court. Another sexual harassment case came forward that year, but Griffin characterized both as extortion (Anderson 1992).

Buffalo, New York DJ and music business entrepreneur Marty Angelo created the TV show *Disco Step-by-Step*. The first show, hosted by Angelo, was aired on cable on January 1, 1977. After six months, the network affiliate Channel 4 picked it up for the fall season.

Taping took place, from late 1975 through 1976, in various upstate discos. The show consisted of two 10-minute dance lessons led by professional Buffalo instructors and between the lessons, "experienced" people danced the New York Hustle, the Latin Hustle, or Salsa. Angelo would introduce a new record. Guests danced to it and then voted to "Make It or Break It," after which Angelo would either add it to a future playlist or physically break it. (At the decade end, button-wearing extremists would copy this to revile all of disco.) The one-hour show also had a "Disco Spotlight" featuring couples and a "Disco Profile" celebrity guest. Chic, the Bee Gees, Grace Jones, Silver Convention, and Cerrone appeared either in person or via video.

Disco Step-by-Step promoted *Saturday Night Fever* before its release. In that episode, guests (some dressed in Travolta or Gorney costumes) danced to the Bee Gees' "More than a Woman." Cutaways showed clips of Travolta and Gorney dancing in the upcoming film.

The show claimed over 400,000 weekly viewers. Seventy-three shows aired, of 48 original sessions, until January 15, 1980. Angelo succumbed to the drugs available in the entertaining life. After serving two years of a six-year prison sentence for cocaine possession, he formed Marty Angelo Ministries. Its Web site reaches out to troubled celebrities, prison inmates, and drug addicts.

The early dance shows removed disco's gay content, but as audiences grew more tolerant, the new reality dance shows grew more "real." MTV and VH1 featured controversial, interesting lifestyles. *Dancing with the Stars* sought to attract viewers by pairing actors and other celebrities with professional dancers. *American Idol* and *So You Think You Can Dance* are highly competitive and extremely popular shows that bring dance into our living rooms and continue the tradition of armchair dancing.

Fame

This engaging 1980 musical is about student hopefuls at New York City's High School of Performing Arts. The filming took place during the summer of 1979 in the abandoned Haaren High School, west of the Theater District. British director Alan Parker revived it with movie set interiors. Irene Cara won the Best Actress Academy Award as Coco and performs the Michael and Leslie Gore song "Out There on My

Own," which was nominated for Best Song. The modern dance choreographer Louis Falco made his film debut with *Fame*.

For the film's most famous, big, and rowdy dance number, a music
student befriends Cara's bold character and surprises everyone with
the hit "Fame." (It did win the Academy Award for Best Song and a
Golden Globe Award for Best Original Song.) His taxi-driver father
plays it from stereo loudspeakers atop his cab, parked outside the
school entrance (actually a church doorway opposite the Forty-sixth
High School of Performing Arts). The jubilant dance stops traffic.
Groups of kids storm the street performing similar, stretched, and airborne choreography. The effect is release and jouissance. Falco and the
cast made the dance to Donna Summer's "Hot Stuff" and added
"Fame" after the shoot.

"Hot Lunch Jam" is a jazzy number in which the lunchroom turns
into a disco. Cara sings, resembling a young Donna Summer. Kids play
instruments, and the dancing breaks out, including raggedy line
dances, kids dancing singly on top of the piano and on the floor, and a
disco couple bumping. Even the lunchroom monitor is dancing low to
the ground, monitoring the progress of his jack-in-the-box ambulation.

There are lovely inside views of the ballet classes and a scene with
top student Antonia Franceschi practicing her adagio. She flirts with
the dance star, Leroy, played by Gene Anthony Ray who actually did
attend the High School of Performing Arts (for a year). Parker found
him dancing on a Harlem street corner. Parker auditioned thousands
of teens in his extensive auditioning process. Most had no acting
experience.

The story begins with an audition required for admission to the
school. The teachers (including Debbie Allen in a cameo appearance)
love Leroy's hot dance, and he wins the placement. Shirley Mulholland
(Carol Massenburg) brought him along as a partner in her routine. She
wanted to learn how to dance. She stomps out in her orange platform
shoes after he upstages her, and we do not see her again. We see
plenty of him as he struggles to surmount challenges he was ill
prepared for.

Parker packed the film with his fascination for the time and place.
The film's subplots include coming of age and sexual awakening in
the gritty city. It was part of a rash of yearly, major, musical classics,
following *Saturday Night Fever* and *Grease*. Parker says in his DVD
commentary that *Fame* is a documentary pushed to its theatrical limits.

In a movie-within-a-movie scene, drama students played by Maureen Teefy and Barry Miller (who plays the suicidal Bobby C. in *Saturday Night Fever*) go to one of the Tuesday midnight screenings of *Rocky Horror Picture Show*. In 1979, audiences created ritualistic theater at an East Village movie house (and at 50 others around the nation). They attended week after week dressed as the film characters and carrying small props. The audience knew the lines and recited them en masse, adding unison gestures. For example, in a dark rainy night scene, the moviegoers covered their heads with open newspapers. They rolled their heads with the instructional group "Time Warp Dance" in the film.

Allen and Ray return in the subsequent 1982 TV series, *Fame*, which ran for five years and stoked the fire for the original. Ray died at 41 in 2003. He was HIV positive and had a fatal stroke. Parker directed an updated *Fame*, but it disappointed devotees of the first, timeless version.

Epilogue

I find something annoying about the mentality of those who keep han-
dling the goods while denying any appetite for them.
　　　　　　　—Harold Rosenberg, "Pop Culture: Kitsch Criticism"

Boundaries of all kinds blurred in the 1970s. People even questioned
whether disco was good clean fun or bad art. The trouble came in the
affixing of labels and morals to disco dancing (meaning dancing in discos to disco music). For a myriad of reasons, people turned against
disco and dancing too. Their disillusion came to a head in 1979, but it
had been fomenting for several years.

　In 1977, a homicidal nut went on a rampage killing and injuring
young couples. He left scary letters to police and media. In the first
he said, "The wemon [*sic*] of Queens are the prettiest . . . ," and signed
it "Son of Sam." After the news that the victims had long, brown hair,
women cut and dyed theirs or stayed in. The mood was one of
strangely deadened and quieted innocence. The owner of the club
Elephas turned the kids away that summer. Some New Yorkers
recalled the prohibition-era moral myth that "The Dance Hall Is Hell's
Ante-Room" (Giordano 2008).

　A few years later, the gay cancer was wiping out disco dancers. That
led to more moralizing and misplaced fear mongering. However,
when it took the name AIDS, people danced in proactive protest. They

Elephas, 1977. (Associated Press)

organized parties to raise money and morale. The outpouring helped the victims directly and benefited research and education efforts.

Susan Sontag came to reject camp. Other queer theorists rejected "Notes on Camp" for its black and white definitions. It gave agency and visibility to homosexuals by granting them special access to rhythm and musicality. But stereotyping homosexuals, blacks, or Latinos was counterproductive to the disco ideal that dancing is for everybody.

Although disco brought people of different races and classes together, they found that dancing together (sometimes) in clubs did not always result in breaking down barriers. It took a long time to build animosity between peoples, and the repair work had only begun. *Saturday Night Fever* brought disco's segregation to light.

Disco dancing followed the music. Dancing had to do with feeling the music; the music had to have feeling. Not dancing in discos followed the perception of declining quality in the music. At the end of the 1970s, record labels were racing to grab talent. In the flood of new product, more good stuff was produced, and more stuff that was impersonal and uninspiring. Detractors harshly criticized the bad stuff and called it "disco."

Rocker Frank Zappa parodied disco dancers in "Dancin' Fool" on his *Sheik Yerbouti* album. Rick Dees's *Disco Duck* is a disco cartoon. Many dancers could no longer suspend disbelief. The bubble pierced when *Saturday Night Fever* brought the song to light. The silly duckbill on the LP cover represented all that people rejected about disco.

On the dance floor, everyone came to be a star. With so many glowing, the scene became discordant. It tore the fabric of togetherness that was disco's innocent aim. This mass megalomania helped bring forth the fall of disco. Disco came down like the users of cocaine, "poppers," and crystal meth or the greedy club owners, cops, and the mob.

People blamed Giorgio Moroder for turning Hollywood with *Flashdance*. John Travolta took blame when he decamped from Hustle and went Western in *Urban Cowboy*. Some blamed the music. Others faulted the dance styles themselves, which had multiplied ridiculously and confusingly. When Hustle aspired to Hollywood virtuosity, the average fun-seeker was not willing or able to compete.

Considering all this, it is still hard to fathom the hatred that so many Americans directed at dancers in clubs and dance music, but yes, nationwide riots ensued. For decades, the Hustle and the word disco were absent from vocabularies, and the era disappeared from revisionist history. Archives preserved little or no evidence.

Disco Sucks (Disco as Effigy)

On July 13, 1979, rock radio WLUP DJ Steve Dahl and his listeners stormed a game in Chicago's Comiskey Park. The White Sox were hosting the Detroit Tigers in a double header. Dahl had been hired to plan and preside over a half-time promotion to increase teen attendance. He had rallied his radio listeners for a Disco Demolition event by blowing up records with sound effects on his show, in the days preceding the game. Each person entering the stadium with a disco record to burn got to see the game for only 98 cents. The crowd exceeded expectations, at around 45,000, with approximately 20,000 turned away at the entrance.

When Dahl ignited the container of records in the middle of the playing field, fans jumped out of their seats to join him, tearing up the grass. They brought more of their collections to set ablaze in smaller, outlying fires. It took an hour to get the situation under control. Security was inadequate. Authorities of the playing field declared the field unfit and cancelled the second game. The scoreboard read, "Get ready for the disco demolition between games" and then "Please return to your seats."

KAZY-FM of Denver had a similar anti-disco on-air game. Listeners called in and named their least favorite disco song, and the DJ would simulate its destruction with sound effects. The motto of KROQ-FM from Pasadena was "abolish disco in our lifetime." An anti-disco vigilante group called Disco Ducks Klan had an intelligence arm called DREAD or Detroit Rockers Engaged in the Abolition of Disco. The group collected names and phone numbers of disco lovers and performed mock executions on WRIF. XLO-FM, New York, had a "no Bee Gees" weekend in 1978 and also planned a "no disco" weekend for 1979. Dahl called his demonstration "an ultimate victory." The campaign spread to some rock 'n roll bars and record stores, and seemingly normal young people wore sew-on patches and buttons with the slogan "disco sucks." Some music industry professionals predicted future embarrassment over the demonstration (McIntyre 1979).

David McGee, writing in *Record World*'s New York, NY Column, likened the demonstration to the burning of rock records in the 1950s and Beatle records in the 1960s. "Is Dahl so narrow-minded as to believe that disco music is endangering the future of rock music?" Like rock, disco is here to stay, he said (McGee 1979).

Nevertheless, when disco was deemed dead, records were destroyed or suddenly scarce on store shelves. Disco came to represent all that was wrong with the world and, mainly, its commercialism. The new Disco File writer Brian Chin reported in a November 1979 *Record World* article that labels, DJs, and the DJ record pool For the Record, headed by Judy Weinstein, were using the term "DOR" or "dance oriented rock" to usher in a broader crop of new, danceable songs. Chin diplomatically kept up disco's mantle after the violent backlash.

If a handful of radio rock DJs had mobilized against disco, then there were at least that many club and radio DJs who were keeping disco alive, in its classic form as something precious and rare. Disco outlived its unpopularity because it persisted as a path to sociality, empowerment, and pleasure. Undeniable quality found in the music and dancing of the era continues to inspire.

Disco Wanted Dead or Alive

When people turned against disco, the music and dancing did not stop in gay dance halls. Furthermore, gays did not feel that the backlash was directed toward them. They had lived with taunting. The association of disco with homosexuality strengthened, since gay people were still dancing, underground. Openly gay was still not the norm.

Meanwhile, rap gained popularity. Rappers wanted to reassert their manhood after feeling that disco had undermined and questioned it. A new toughness and steely gleam replaced disco's warm fuzziness. Michael Jackson assimilated it in "Beat It."

Many went underground where the dancing never stopped. The message of "I Will Survive" took on more, rather than less, importance. In the 1970s, the act of surviving was heroic and worthy of celebration, said Greil Marcus in his 1989 *Lipstick Traces: A Secret History of the 20th Century*. In the following decades, surviving became the new Life. Weeklong parties, drugs, and promiscuous sex were not so practical. But dancing could live on. When the dust settled on the Comiskey Park debacle, and this took several decades, Americans wondered what all the fuss was. They took out the disco records and found new and old dance halls "where the happy people go."

People had new hope for the disco ideals of unity in 2008 when President Obama was elected. A campaign against childhood obesity was already under way. Dancing went along with the push for self-improvement, fitness, and fun. This was also a time of transparency and (electronic) connection. It served Obama-age revelers who cheaply, easily, and instantly gathered dancers and information about dances and music.

In an April 2009 *New Yorker* article, Sasha Frere-Jones called Lady Gaga disco. Could she have emerged without Madonna? The kids called Gaga electro-pop. Nonetheless, the assertiveness that performing, dancing 1970s women clumsily sought looks refined in the new millennium. Studies show significant gains in the self-confidence, vanity, and self-importance of Generation Y women (Carey 2010).

The Martinez Brothers are twenty-first century DJs who wanted to bring the Paradise Garage and Loft ethic to Manhattan Clubs. They played at Cielo in 2009. Hercules and Love Affair, Holy Ghost!, Glass Candy, Horsemeat Disco, and LCD Soundsystem are new musical groups for the new generation of dancers. "Disco never died," said DJ Michel Gaubert to Alex Hawgood in *T Magazine*; "It has only become more acceptable" (Hawgood 2008).

People dress up or down to go out to new dance halls in West Harlem and downtown. Against the Gowanus Canal backwind, Bklyn Yard holds a silent disco (the patrons are plugged into iPods). It hosts Sunday Best, an afternoon party for dancers with day jobs. Été d'Amour was launched in 2008 at Santos Party House. It moved to the Lower Eastside Rivington Hotel, where the Parisian DJ Dmitri spins from 1 p.m. to 1 a.m. on Sundays. Susanne Bartsch sends weekly evites for Sundays at Greenhouse. Sunday parties are popular, twenty-first-century extensions of disco-era Tea parties, which are more popular than ever in gay circles. White Parties continue, seemingly at any time of year. Hustle competitions dot the calendar and the country. In 2008, 7,000 people danced at Buffalo's yearly World's Largest Disco event. Dances of the era survive.

The Hustle transcended the disco era and continues as the latest partner dance that adapts ballroom, Latin, and black jazzy styles to current, up-tempo dance music. In the 1970s, Italian-American men, Jewish women, and other young working people emulated the dancing example of Latinos, especially the men. It was a time of healing through dance for men of all persuasions. The dance was named Hustle because of the quick shifts in direction, flicking wrists and feet, and purposeful, walk-around conversation between partners. Cuban arrivals in Florida Cha-Cha-ed to disco music, but many would agree that Hustle is the unofficial, quintessential New York City dance. (The official New York State dance is the Lindy Hop.)

Hustle's persistence is surprising because Hustle dancers, the ones who knew all the steps, were the very targets of the cooler-than-thou, button or patch-wearing "disco sucks" rockers and punk rockers, who were seeking music with more intellectual or literary substance. They needed a new kind of rebellion. They wanted to listen, groove, jump, and rave. They were unable to find individuality in the steps everyone was doing on the dance floor. They preferred a less-demanding kind of participation.

Meanwhile, disco dancers longed for the days when people used to dance and sweat. They missed the romance. Many tuned in to *Dancing with the Stars*. Others went to the Y, to the studios, and to the clubs, and made their own fun. The THP Orchestra had it right with their perpetually danceable 1979 club hit "Dancing Forever." We keep dancing. Ashford & Simpson too predicted it that year in "Dance Forever." Everyone on the floor knew the dancing would go on.

Bibliography

Albright, Ann Cooper. *Traces: Absence and Presence in the Work of Loie Fuller*. Middletown, CT: Wesleyan University Press, 2007.

Aletti, Vince. "I Won't Dance, Don't Ask Me." *Village Voice*, April 26, 1976.

Aletti, Vince. "The Loft." *Village Voice*, June 16, 1975.

Aletti, Vince. *The Disco Files: 1973–78*. London: Djhistory.com, 2009.

Alexander, Ron. "Hustling Off to Dance Classes. " *New York Times*, December 1, 1981.

Allen, Derrick, interview by Lori Ortiz, September 5, 2009.

Allen, Derrick, interview by Ron Bess, rhythmlounge.tv, June 10, 2008.

Amante, Robin, interview by Lori Ortiz, September 6, 2009.

Anderson, Roger. "Seen, Heard, Said." *Seattle Times*, January 8, 1992.

Angelo, Marty, interview by Gene Arnold, *Disco History-Part 3*. giantgene.com, (ca.2000). http://www.soul-patrol.net/disco3.ram.

Apple. "Larry Levan." itunes.apple.com.

Associated Press. "N.Y. Court Upholds Cabaret Law." *USA Today*, February 23, 2007.

Avant-Garde, Aaron. "Kevin Ultra Omni." *Cut Magazine*, October 1992.

Baumgold, Julie. "The Exotic Merchant of the Night." *New York Magazine*, March 21, 1977: 37–45.

Bego, Mark and Randy Jones. *Macho Man: The Disco Era and Gay America's "Coming Out."* Westport, CT: Praeger, 2009.

Bess, Ron, interview by Lori Ortiz, July 2010.

Bess, Ron. "Hustle Hall of Fame." mjames.org. Mark James, n.d.

Bess, Ron. "Vincent Montana, Jr." *Mark James Dance Zone*. July 20, 2004.

Billboard. "A Rosy Picture for Roller Rinks." *Billboard Magazine*, August 11, 1979: 56.

Billboard. "N.J. Park Becomes Disco Dream World. " *Billboard Magazine*, August 4, 1979: 44.

Birmingham, Nan. "Why We're Dancing Again. " *Town & Country*, March 1976: 57.

Bleyer, Jennifer. "The Last Lace-Up." *New York Times*, April 22, 2007.

Bloom, Ken. *Broadway: An Encyclopedia*. New York, NY: Routledge, 2004.

Boyle, Donna, interview by Lori Ortiz, May 4, 2009.

Braunstein, Peter. "Disco." *American Heritage* 50, Issue 7 (November 1999): 43–54.

Brewster, Bill and Frank Broughton. *Last Night A DJ Saved My Life*. New York, NY: Grove Press, 1999.

Bromley, Scott, interview by Lori Ortiz, December 16, 2008.

Bronson, Fred. *Billboard Number 1 Hits*. New York, NY: Billboard Books, 2003.

Brown, James. *I Feel Good*. New York, NY: New American Library, 2005.

Caldwell, Jennifer and James Harney. "It's Dance Night: Harvest Moon Ball Marks 50th." *NY Daily News*, October 21, 1984.

Canby, Vincent. "Roseland (1977) Film Festival: 'Roseland' Casts Spell over Lonely Fox-Trotters. " *New York Times*, October 2, 1977.

Carey, Benedict. "A Snapshot of a Generation May Come Out Blurry." *New York Times*, August 3, 2010: D5.

Carroll, Billy, interview by Lori Ortiz, 2008.

Carroll, Maurice. "An Unlikely Setting for a Violent Crime." *New York Times*, June 27, 1977.

Cheren, Mel. *My Life and the Paradise Garage*. New York, NY: Twenty-four Hours for Life, 2000.

Chin, Brian, *The Disco Box*. Rhino Entertainment Company, 1999.

ChuckB. "Uncle Sam's." Discomusic.com, August 31, 2004.

Cohn, Nik. "Tribal Rites of the New Saturday Night." *New York Magazine*, June 7, 1976.

Conrad, Neil, interview by Lori Ortiz, November 2008.

Cornelius, Don, interview by Time-Life. *The Best of Soul Train*, DVD, 2010.

Currie, Cherie. *Neon Angel*. New York, NY: Harper Collins, 2010.

Diebold, David. *Tribal Rites*. San Francisco, CA: Time Warp Publishing, 1986.

Dmitri. "Get Down with the Philly Sound." YouTube. Bbe Press. April 10, 2010.

Donald, Uncle. "A Tribute to Toad Hall." theCastro.net. April 1, 1998.

Douglas, Barry. "Hustle." Victor Eijkhout. Eijkhout.net. October 17, 1999.

Dyer, Richard. "In Defence of Disco." *Gay Left* 8, Summer 1979: 20–23.

Ebony. "The 'Outrageous' Waack." August 1978: 64–66.

Echols, Alice. *Hot Stuff: Disco and the Remaking of American Culture*. New York, NY: W.W. Norton & Co., 2010.

English, Camper. "Thirty Years of the EndUp." *San Francisco Bay Guardian*. November 5, 2003.

Estien, Julio, interview by Lori Ortiz, July 2010.

Fajardo, Billy, interview by Lori Ortiz, September 4, 2009.

Fajardo, Billy. "History of the Dance." i-h-d-a.com (International Hustle Dance Association).

Fichera, Salvatore, interview by Lori Ortiz, November 2008.

Gamson, Joshua. "Milk Marched to a Disco Beat." filmsinfocus.com, November 21, 2008.

Gamson, Joshua. *The Fabulous Sylvester: The Legend, the Music, the Seventies in San Francisco*. New York, NY: Henry Holt and Company, 2005.

Gaynor, Gloria. "I Will Survive." YouTube. Wesley Tai and Polydor, 1979.

Gaynor, Gloria, interview by Gene Arnold. "The Sounds of Philly." *Gene Arnold Superstar Concert*. Infinity Broadcasting. Joy Radio Network, New York, 1979.

Giordano, Ralph G. *Satan in the Dance Hall*. New York, NY: Scarecrow Press, 2008.

Giordano, Ralph G.. *Social Dancing in America*. Westport, CT: Greenwood, 2007.

Goldman, Albert. *Disco*. New York, NY: Hawthorn Books, 1978.

Graham, Samuel. "Some Anti-Disco Promotions Go On Despite WLUP's Baseball Disaster." *Record World*, July 1979.

Grasso, Francis, interview by Frank Broughton. DJ History.com, April 2, 1999.

Green, Marion, interview by Lori Ortiz, July 13, 2010.

Green, Marion. "Village Skating." http://web.me.com/roxydjjulio/NYC_DJ_Julio/Village_Skating.html.

Grigoriadis, Vanessa. "Regine's Last Stand." *New York Magazine,* April 12, 1999.

Haber, Deborah. "Disco Dancing: The Snaky New Steps." *New York Magazine*, November 29, 1976.

Hawgood. "Now Spinning | A Disco Beat." *T Magazine*, 2008: 80.

Helgesen, Sally. "Disco." *Harper's*, October 1977: 20–24.

Holden, Stephen. "Shadow Dancing." *Rolling Stone*, August 24, 1978.

Hughes, Walter. "Feelin' Mighty Real: Disco as Discourse and Discipline." *Village Voice Rock & Roll Quarterly,* July 13, 1993.

IHDA. "Who's Who Spotlight." I-h-d-a.com, n.d.

IMBD. "Mary Tyler Moore." imbd.com, n.d.

Isherwood, Christopher. *The World in the Evening*. New York, NY: Farrar, Straus & Giroux, 1952.

Jacobs, Andrew. "Heaven on Wheels." *New York Times*, November 30, 2005.

Jacobs, Jody. "L.A. on the Disco Bandwagon." *Los Angeles Times*, May 17, 1978: F2.

Jefferson, Margo. *On Michael Jackson*. New York, NY: Vintage Books, 2006.

Jett, Joan, interview by Katie Rich. "Sundance Interview: Joan Jett." Cinema Blend.com.

Johnston, Laurie. "City Gets Caught Up in the Roller-Skating Whirl." *New York Times*, September 1, 1980: B1.

Jones, Grace. *Tomorrow.* Recorded by Bobby Viteritti. January 29, 1977.

Jordan, Jim. "FIQNews Interview with Dominick Desantis." Fireislandqnews.com.

Joseph, Ron, interview by Gene Arnold. *Disco History-Part 3.* giantgene.com (ca. 2000).

Judge, Diane. "Don De Natale, the Prince of Dance Calls Roseland His Home." *New York Post*, April 7, 1981.

Kashner, Sam. "Fever Pitch: When Travolta Did Disco; the Making of *Saturday Night Fever.*" In *Best Music Writing 2008*, edited by Nelson George, 236–260. Philadelphia, PA: Da Capo Press, 2008.

Kelly, Raymond, interview by Sewell Chan. "30 Years Since Son of Sam." cityroom.blogs.nytimes.com, August 6, 2007.

Kopkind, Andrew. "The Dialectic of Disco." In *Thirty Years' War*, 317. New York, NY: Verso, 1995.

Lauren, Jena. *Disco*. Los Angeles, CA: Price, Stern, Sloan, 1979.

Lawrence, Tim. *Love Saves the Day*. New York, NY: Duke University Press, 2005.

LeBash, hotdiscomix/Jack/Terence S./Phil. "Le Jardin." Disco-disco.com.

Leslie, Robbie. Archived notes. Email interview by Lori Ortiz, April 20, 2010.

LGBT Community Center Archive. *Rollerena Fairy Godmother Collection*, New York City.

Lopez, Bernard. DiscoMusic.com. 2002.

Lustgarten, Karen, phone interview by Lori Ortiz, November 15, 2009.

Lustgarten, Karen. *Disco Dancing*. New York, NY: Warner Books, 1978.

MacNeil, Robert. "Art and Freedom." pbs.org. July 3, 2005.

Madrid, Roy. *Disco . . . You Should Be Dancing!* Los Angeles, CA: Multi-Media Marketing, 1978.

Mangels, Andy. "The Village People Story." *Can't Stop the Music Extra*. DVD. Anchor Bay Entertainment. 2002.

Martin, Gavin. "1993: Slayed in Fame." In *The Faber Book of Pop*, by Hanif Kureishi and Jon Savage. London: Faber and Faber, 1995.

Maslin, Janet. "Screen: The Prince of Bay Ridge." *New York Times*, December 16, 1977.

McGee, David. "New York, NY." *Record World*, July 28, 1979.

McIntyre, Neil. "WLUP and Steve Dahl Are Unfazed in the Aftermath of Anti-Disco Riot." *Record World*, July 28, 1979: 1.

McLaughlin, Mark. *Disco: Spinning the Story*. June 7, 2005.

Morley, Paul. "Vince Aletti, Bill Brewster, and Luke Howard." *Guardian*, August 20, 2009.

Needs, Kris. "The Runaways: The Runaways." *Rock's Back Pages*, September 1976.

Nentl, Jerolyn Ann. *Disco Dancing*. Minneapolis, MN: Crestwood House, 1980.

Nieves, Evelyn. "Noisy Discos Are Targets of Crackdown." *New York Times*, August 20, 1990.

Orodenker, Maurie. "Philly DJ Blavat Taping Own Syndicated Disco Show." *Billboard*, February 17, 1979: 24.

Pareles, Jon. "José Fajardo, 82, Flutist and Bandleader, Is Dead." *New York Times*, December 20, 2001.

Peck, Abe. *Dancing Madness*. Garden City, NY: Rolling Stone Press, 1976.

Picture, Bill. *EndUp*. *San Francisco Chronicle*, February 19, 2006.

Pollack, Bruce. *The Disco Handbook*. New York, NY: Scholastic Books, 1979.

Popper, Ben. "Moonwalker: A History of Michael Jackson's Signature Move." Obit-mag.com, June 26, 2009.

Post, Henry. "The Front." *New York Magazine*, December 4, 1978.

Pugliese, Joseph, interview by Izzy Sanabria. *Latin NY Magazine*, February 78, 33.

Ramos, Josell. *Maestro*. DVD. 2003.

Ramsdell, Ronald, interview by Lori Ortiz, November 2008.

Rauh, Grace. "Mayor May Overhaul or Repeal Cabaret Law." *New York Sun*, July 15, 2008.

Rella, Nancyann. "Dancing Still a Ball for Them." *Yonkers Statesman*, September 19, 1974.

RobertIII, bigbadblazer77 a.k.a. *Do The Hustle*. YouTube. December 7, 2007.

Robertson, Frank. "Disco Tech." In *Dancing Madness*, by Abe Peck, 27–29. Garden City, NY: Rolling Stone Press, 1976.

Rollerena, interview by Lori Ortiz, July 26, 2010.

Romano, Tricia. "Roxy Music." *Village Voice*, March 6, 2007.

Rosenberg, Harold. "Pop Culture: Kitsch Criticism." In *The Tradition of the New*, 259–268. New York, NY: Horizon Press, 1959.

Rosenberg, Jessica and Gitana, Garafolo. "Riot Grrrl: Revolutions from Within." *Journal of Women in Culture and Society* (University of Chicago) 23, no. 3 (1988).

Saint, The. "Interview with Bruce Mailman Owner of the Saint." myspace.com, March 31, 2007.

Salazar, Max. "Remembering the Corso." *Latin Beat Magazine,* September 2000.

Sanabria, Bobby. "Tito Puente: Long Live the King." lpmusic.com, June 2000.

Settimelli, Michael Terrace and Peter. "Palladium-House-of-Mambo." *Que Pasa Magazine*, September 19, 2007.

Shapiro, Peter. *Turn the Beat Around*. New York, NY: Farrar, Straus and Giroux, 2005.

Shapiro, Steve. "The Shapiro Files." shapsteve.blogspot.com, December 24, 2006.

Silano, Steve, interview by Lori Ortiz, December 2008.

Sommers, Sally. "C'mon to My House." *Dance Research Journal* 33, no. 2 (Winter 2001).

Sontag, Susan. "Notes on Camp." In *Against Interpretation*, by Susan Sontag. New York, NY, 1961.

Sparkletack, Richard. "Today in San Francisco History—The Black Cat Café." sfist.com, October 31, 2008.

Tai, Wesley. "I Will Survive." Polygram. *YouTube*, May 21, 2007. http://www .youtube.com/watch?v=ZBR2G-iI3-I (accessed 2010).

Terrio, Deney. *Night Moves*. K-tel, 1979.

The Broadcast Pioneers of Philadelphia. "Ron Joseph, A Broadcast Pioneer." http://www.broadcastpioneers.com/rj.html (accessed May 6, 2010).

The Modesto Bee. "Barry Gibb reflects of the Bee Gees' Success." *The Modesto Bee*, November 17, 1979: 26.

VH1. "VH1 Classic All-Time Top 10: Michael Jackson." http://www.vh1.com/ video/michael-jackson/13322/thriller.jhtml#id=1630515 V (accessed June 5, 2010).

Viteritti, Bobby, interviews by Lori Ortiz, May 2010.

Wandel, Rich. "The Saint". New York: unpublished.

White Light Productions. remembertheparty.com, 2009.

Whiting, Sam. "It's 7 a.m.—Time to Dance." *sfgate.com*, February 19, 2006.

Williams, Jean. "Growing Disco Scene." *Billboard*, March 19, 1977: 18.

Williams, Ron. "San Francisco before Stonewall." *webcastro.com*. 1995.

Winders, James A. *Paris Africain: Rhythms of the African Diaspora*. New York, NY: Palgrave MacMillan, 2006.

Index

About the Author

Lori Ortiz is a New York City–based journalist. Her articles about dance have appeared in New York City weeklies and art and dance trade journals, including *DANCE, Pointe,* the *Village Voice, PAJ: A Journal of Performance and Art,* and Artcritical.com. Lori reviewed dance regularly for *Gay City News* from 2004 to 2008. She grew up in Brooklyn and New Jersey and studied art, music, and dance, earning a BFA in painting from Alfred University. She is the publisher of ReadingDance.com. This is her first book.